NO CONTACT SU

Escaping a lifetime of

by Alice Little

To my husband who reminds me that unconditional love and
kindness exists

To all survivors of abuse everywhere

To all the people I met in my life whether it was a good or bad
connection. Each connection taught me a lot about myself.

Alice Little is a survivor of parental sexual, ritual and narcissistic abuse within a paedophile community. She has spent over 30 years studying various therapies and spiritual traditions on her own journey of self development, including a three year Tibetan Buddhist retreat. In order to heal she had no choice but to go 'No Contact' with her toxic abusive parents, family, husband, town, home,spiritual group and friends for the rest of her life, forever.

The advice in this book is given in good faith based on the experiences of the author. The reader should not rely on it alone and is advised to seek further professional help. Any use of information in this book is at the reader's discretion and risk. Neither the author nor the publisher can be held responsible for any loss, claim or damage arising out of the use, or misuse, of the suggestions made, the failure to take medical advice or for any material on third party websites.

Dear reader

If you are reading this now I know you may be depressed, sad, confused and even, perhaps, have mental or physical problems. You may be sure or unsure and are questioning if you may have suffered at the hands of an evil Narcissist. If so, this also tells me that you are a kind, loving and caring human being. That's why they chose you. I also know that you want to be healed, be happy and find joy and peace from your suffering and that is why you are reading and researching this subject. You must be in so much pain and I can't hug you in person so I am sending you a virtual one with this book.

You are so brave. You have been through so much and still you are a warm-hearted human being. It's just that you are suffering. You can heal, it is possible. I don't mean you will be happy every day, forever, but your emotions will be less intense and the memories and pictures in your mind will eventually fade. You may not believe that right now because you are behind the door that you will eventually walk though, the door marked life, freedom and joy.

Some days you will be exhausted as you look at your past, so exhausted that you just have to lie down. Then when you do lie down you realise that you are so exhausted you can't even rest or sleep. This battle that you are fighting is the warrior's path. You are in training to see how strong you really are!

It may seem that there is no end and no future but that is the mirage, the blocked door that stops you from seeing what is beyond. There will always be other doors because you have chosen the warrior's path, but each door will get easier and soon you will enjoy closing them behind you.

I have been on this path a very long time so I have some idea of what it's like at the beginning. I also know what it's like further along the path. Life changes after No Contact. First the hard bit when you go into a deep period of grief and fight hard not to go back to those toxic people. Then you get past that point and you wonder why you ever stayed so long. You have to begin again and

5

you may be alone with your healing, with no support, but you are not alone. There are many of us treading this path. We don't walk it through choice. We do so because we have no choice.

Your path is to win the best prize of all, control of your own mind and life. Taking back your own power that was taken from you by the narcissists in your life.

We are amazing! Why? Because we can and want to change. The narcissist will never change.

Alice

CONTENTS

PART 1. Going 'No contact'

PART 2. Healing a lifetime of depression and abuse.

PART 3. Life as a spiritual journey beyond religion

Introduction

This book is based on my own experience as a survivor of sexual, emotional, narcissistic abuse by my parents, family, friends, community and partners. I have found in my own experience and research the following:-

In order to be able to hurt a vulnerable child you have to take away empathy and care.

If it's your own child you have to be devoid of any paternal instincts.

To cross the boundary and sexually abuse your child you have to be a person who has been degraded or brainwashed and is capable of degrading another.

If you sell your child for money in exchange for adults to have sex with that child, you have to take away your humanity and shame or guilt.

To do all three you would have to be a parent or person with Narcissistic Personality Disorder. (NPD)

In showing your child or a child that they are worthless you set them up to meet future Narcissists. A cycle of trans-generational abuse has been passed on.

To groom an adult for the purpose of sex you have to be a predator unable to see the person beyond their bodies which you intend to use for your own selfish desires.

To groom an adult for the purpose of prostitution you have to be part of a group who does this and knows who to target.

To use a prostitute for the purpose of sex you have to be a person who prefers to enjoy sex without intimacy.

To be a prostitute you have to think that all you are desirable for is your body.

To have been groomed as a prostitute you have to have been a survivor of childhood abuse whether you remember that or not.

If you visit a prostitute the chances are that you are having sex with an adult abuse victim who may be trapped as a slave to a pimp.

If you are into child sexual abuse and paedophilia you will be also drawn to, or are part of, a bestiality network.

If you are part of a bestiality network you will also be drawn into, or are part of, human or animal sacrifice in the form of Ritual Abuse. (RA)

If you are part of a Ritual Abuse network you are probably part of a secret society and are at the bottom of a big ladder which you may or may not be able to climb.

If you are part of a secret society whatever its name you are not human. You have sold your soul to be where you are.

You may or may not agree with the above opinions but they are based on my own experience and the experience of other survivors that I have come into contact with.

Not everyone carries on as an abuser because of abuse done to them. I certainly did not. Some are made to abuse others as part of a technique of brainwashing making them complicit in the act. There are those who have been abused and do not recover at all from such trauma and there are those who, like myself, survive despite what was done to them. There is a price to pay in the form of physical and mental health issues and life choices.

When I say I went 'No Contact' I don't just mean I left my family. I mean I left absolutely everything. I lost my home, career, friends, family, spiritual group and last of all I left myself, the self I was when I was living with bullying abusive, narcissistic people. After a lifetime of sexual, mental and physical Narcissistic Abuse from my family, ex-husband, community and friends I was left with no choice but to leave everything behind and go 'No Contact' FOREVER!

This was not a decision that I wanted to do but rather stemmed from a sense of self-preservation. It is not a decision to be taken lightly because even when you have gone No Contact there is then the fall out from such a huge life changing decision.

I have had my life and everything in it taken from me time and time again by my parents and encounters with narcissists I met in my life. Sweeping everything away with a hand stroke they evicted me from my life, leaving me destitute.

This book is a memoir of short stories of my life and how I finally went No Contact. What effect that had on me and how I coped and cope with it now. Because I have gone No Contact with my abusers I am only able to tell some of my story in order to stay as I am, away from them. I never, ever, ever, ever want to have anything to do with those in my past and to do so I guard my freedom however I need to. This means that this is only a fraction of what really happened to me.

This book is divided into three parts:

Part 1 deals with my realisation that my parents had serious personality disorders in the form of NPD. I recount short stories regarding this and also give contemplations at the end of each chapter to aid the reader in exploring this most damaging of disorders.

Part 2 explores my lifetime of depression and how the cruelty in my childhood including sexual, emotional, ritual narcissistic abuse created this. I also reveal how going No Contact with everything in my past helped to lift this depression to help me move on in my life.

Part 3 integrates all my life's experiences looking at them as a spiritual path beyond religion. Seeing how my interaction with various therapies and religions touched me on my journey and how I left a long commitment to a Tibetan Buddhist group not long after leaving a three year retreat. How my going No Contact affected my spiritual being and destroyed everything in my life again and again leaving me to start over and over to begin a new life, never being able to settle or find home.

In writing this book I hope that you, the reader, will gain something from my own journey of discovering that my parents had Narcissistic Personality Disorder (NPD) and my journey to recovery and healing.

Instead of feeling there was something wrong with me, my problems stemmed from the fact that there was something deeply wrong with my parent's mental health, in the form of a personality disorder.

My journey to healing and health is constant but having gone 'No Contact' with my parents I am now well beyond that point of no return where the door to my previous life is closed and I have accepted that I will never see my parents again.

As an adult survivor you may have known, deep inside, that something was wrong in the relationship with your parents but thought it was your fault. You may even have been told that directly or indirectly. You may have also suffered in further encounters with narcissists in your life in the form of partners, friends or business colleagues.

I hope you will find something of use to you in reading my story and then I will know my life and the suffering I endured was not in vain.

Contemplations

(guidance on how to use the contemplations for each chapter)

At the end of each chapter I have included thoughts, questions and visualisations for you to contemplate upon.

When you begin your journey find a place where you feel safe and comfortable to open up to very personal things about yourself. If you create a space for yourself which is meaningful to you personally you will be more inspired to be free with your thoughts.

Sit quietly for a while and ask for help from within to create a safe space in which to begin your journey, or invoke whatever represents for you a higher power. Or if that doesn't sound right for you just sit quietly. You could begin the session with some inspiring music or light a candle or incense. What you do in this space is up to you and can be as simple or elaborate as you wish.

When you feel ready read one of the chapters and then go to the contemplation at the end. Ask yourself the questions posed there and then give yourself some time to contemplate on the answers, or sit quietly and do the visualisations. You may like to write the answers down or draw your answer. Do this for every chapter. Keep a journal going with how you are feeling each day noting down any changes you see.

When you come to the end of the book give yourself some time to sit with and realise that you have been very courageous to give yourself the time and space to work on yourself and ask that all the work you do will benefit not only yourself but all beings suffering like yourself.

So take a pen and paper and whatever else you need to make you feel safe and comfortable. Find a space where you will not be disturbed and start your journey of self discovery and freedom. I wish this for you most sincerely.

Alice Little

Suitcase of empty space

My mother took my life away,
in a large tattered old suitcase.
She left only turquoise flowered curtains,
blowing in the wind from the open window.
Scattered lipstick
swept away with an angry hand.
Hints of her perfume in the air
and on her clothes.
Not enough left behind,
to fill my mind.
She left that as empty
as the space she was standing in,
when she waved goodbye.
Case now full,
I was in it.
That space she vacated,
moved into me,
like a creeping disease.
She closed the door that day and took my life,
kept me in that suitcase,
which she preferred
to me.
I'm still in it,
still empty of her
and from her.
I would gladly swap
the turquoise curtains and lipstick
to have her fill that empty space that is me.

Alice Little

PART 1

Going 'No Contact'

My Mother has Narcissistic Personality Disorder

'The devil wears my mother's dress'
Alice Little

When I was a child I had two mothers who both inhabited the same body. One was perfect, loving and kind; the other was a devil. I hid the devil mother away during and after her appearance.

As I became an adult I totally blocked out the bad side of her even though everything indicated that all was not right. It wasn't until I decided to step out of the good girl front that I had put on so that she would approve of me, that the devil mother started to appear again.

This splitting of the good and bad of a care-giver is a well known survival defence mechanism. When I became older the devil mother couldn't hit me so she had to resort to other methods.

My mother's NPD manifested in a way that was very 'crazy-making' because she could also be nice. It wasn't until I started to research NPD that I discovered that this is part of the disorder and her being nice means that she will expect a payback at some stage.

When I was a child her narcissistic rages were huge and could be aroused for doing nothing more than being there. If I was just in her sight there was a possibility that she would give me a slap around the head and then tell me she hated me. But worse than that was when she would suddenly change as if that incident had never just happened and then say she loved me, so my trust was shot.

For many years after I discovered what was wrong with my mother, I could still could be caught up in seeing her as wonderful. I would see her face in my mind or see someone in the street who looked like her and my heart strings would be tugged.

I questioned whether indeed she was bad and that perhaps it was me. Then I would have to remind myself that the imaginary woman I have in my mind, that perfect mother, doesn't exist and it's hard to give that up.

Over time what I have found is that the less I see her as perfect the more I heal. It would be easy to beat myself up and see the nice things she did or feel sorry for the fact that she had a dreadful upbringing too, and I do do that, but then I look at all the wonderful things I did for her and I see that I was in fact the daughter she always wanted, but she could never see that.

The one thing that made up for my lack of mothering was that I spent most of my childhood with my grandmother and she loved me like no one else did. I believe her love saved me and for that she remains forever in my mind and heart.

You may be surprised to know that I love my mother still. I don't know if it's because of the deep roots that her abuse had on me and has or if it's something like Stockholm Syndrome.

The bond we have with our mother can be so strong that they can do anything to us and we, like puppy dogs, love them unconditionally. Sometimes it bothers me when I hear others say how much they hate their mothers wondering why I don't hate mine and other times I feel glad that I don't hate her.

There were also things I liked about my mother and I hope that I take those with me and leave behind the bad traits, or at least be fully aware of any I have copied. But mostly my mother was an imposter who posed as a good mother to the outside world while being cruel when no one was around.

Today as I write this I don't know if my mother or father or my siblings and friends are dead or alive and to free myself I have to let my past go. It must not take over my life now. So instead I look at what I have and I see that my life is at last peaceful. I lead a very simple life and try to be content with what I have instead of what I don't have.

My life could not be more different than it was in even the not too distant past and I see that I have moved on a great deal. There will always be scars and those scars are sometimes opened up but

17

I don't stitch them harshly up, don't indulge in the habits that surround them. Instead I stroke the scars gently and remind myself that if I wouldn't treat a child badly, then how could I possibly do that to the small child that still lives within me. I achieved this by finally admitting that there is something seriously wrong with my parents that can't be talked through or changed.

'My mother and father have Narcissistic Personality Disorder'. Just to admit this was a milestone on my journey, a journey without end. Once you know for sure that it is your parents and family who are indeed mad, and you are not, your healing can begin.

Be aware that your mother has trained you well, in fact your whole childhood has been a psychological minefield in which you have been programmed to please her (impossible) and never question her (dangerous), both of which will drive you mad and never ever work. You can not please her and she is always right, whereas you become a people pleaser and always wrong.

Going No Contact was a serious decision which I felt that I had to take to protect myself and I have to live with the consequences of that every day, but I wouldn't go back, not now, not ever!

Has your mother got NPD?

Contemplation

There are many types of NPD, some borderline and some just downright selfish. My mother was a particular type of narcissist in that she could also be nice, this in itself was very 'crazy-making'. Love (debatable) and hate could be shown within seconds of each other. Other mothers are just nasty all the time. Most of the members of my family were also NPD types but mainly I describe my mother in Part 1 as ours was the most strongest bond and the most destructive to my life.

Narcissism is in all of us and some people are programmed to be selfish but it doesn't mean they have NPD. A personality disorder of this sort is beyond selfish. It means that at some point someone absolutely removed their heart and replaced it with a black heart. NPD people are black hearted with no warm red blood flowing through it. They are just dead and incapable of empathy and love.

If you were raised by one your life would have been terrifying. If you met narcissists afterwards because you were groomed for that purpose by her, chances are that you will be heavily traumatised and most likely will have Post Traumatic Stress even a Complex CPTSD variety. Yet still you might deny that there was something wrong with your mother. Instead you may blame yourself.

So let us explore a few truths to see if your mother had or has NPD. I am sure if you are reading this book you are already suspicious of this fact but just want to verify it.

Here are a few questions to ask yourself:-

- Do you feel like the parent in the relationship?
- Does she deny events that happened?
- Is she disapproving and controlling of your life and choices?
- Do you feel she hates or dislikes you?
- Are you a scapegoat within the family?
- Does your mother have a favourite child? Or a favourite one of your friends?
- Is she inappropriate in what she says or does?
- Has she ever beaten you for no reason?
- Did she ever touch you inappropriately in the guise of nurture?
- Does she have sudden rages?
- Do you find yourself trying to please her?
- Can you never live up to her expectations?

- Do you feel uncomfortable around her.
- Do you feel you are not being yourself?
- Does she *'Gaslight' you by denying your reality?
- Is she different with you in private than she is in public?
- Does she want to always be the centre of attention?

The list is endless and you will find that after reading these more will come to light, write then down.

*Psychological abuse which denies the reality of the victim. The Narcissist will deny their abuse, create scenarios which enable them to unstable you and have you questioning an event that happened but which they deny. This makes you doubt yourself and your world and begin to take their world as yours. Identifying with them, merging with them and finally being so much in their control that you think you are going mad.

Death and Love

One day I will go,
and leave you,
but my love will stay behind forever.
You will feel it in the air,
see it in a smile,
hear it in a song.
You will be my immortality,
you who gave a meaning to my existence,
comforted me in pain,
laughed with me when I tripped.
I have to go you see,
no need to hold back.
Our fingers once clasped tight,
are now in this moment,
broken loose, as I am from this world.
I love you for eternity.

Alice Little

Saying Goodbye, going 'No Contact'

'I would rather live as an outsider and a misfit than fit into the mind of another psychopath'
Alice Little

When I was seven years old my mother just got up and left one day without saying goodbye or taking me with her. This very act haunted me forever and to get over it I shut myself off from any feeling and hid it all inside.

I quickly learned that grown ups didn't hear my cries of mourning and so I hid it even further behind false smiles and pretending that all was OK and I didn't need help. This turned into depression and anxiety and post traumatic stress.

Eventually I lived with my stepmother and father and life was so unbearable with both of them that I ran away several times but no one said anything about it. I was just taken back and the incident forgotten. I even ran away once to my beloved grandmother but she just sent me back and said 'Don't hurt your father'. I was blamed for their abuse of me, denied any help and soon I realised that even my grandmother was not a haven I could run to. I quickly learned that I was on my own, there was no help and no where to run to.

I've spent so much time dealing with the loss of my mother that I never got over it. She blamed me and I, in turn, blamed myself. Both my parents used me to fight each other. It seemed that my mother and I were destined never to be together. Then when I got older I had to say goodbye to her for the last time and left her as she had left me without words to end it. I went No Contact.

Saying goodbye is never easy, especially if it's a forever goodbye, which mine was. I didn't say, "Goodbye, you will never see me again", or have a row and storm out. I just cut off all contact in a final and lasting way, *THE FINAL BOUNDARY.*

I had no choice but to never see her again if I was to heal mentally and physically and my instincts screamed run and don't look back. So I did, I trusted my instincts. It is something women often ignore but this time it came up as a huge warning and I knew if I stayed I would not survive.

It's not a decision to take lightly and some people, instead of going NC, go for minimal contact or contact with boundaries. I longed to see her but I knew in my heart that I wouldn't be seeing the mother I had invented in my mind, I would be seeing instead a woman who, through gritted teeth, would be putting on a smile and saying 'I love you' while plotting her revenge.

Saying goodbye to her meant more than saying goodbye. It also meant goodbye to my home and town, my friends, my job and who I thought I was. Going No Contact can mean breaking contact with everyone who may have a connection with your parents, because if there are any contacts that are in touch with both of you she will use them to be a go between with you and them. She will manipulate them to believe she is good and you are bad, just like she has always done. These people are referred to as 'Flying Monkeys'

I've got so used to my mother walking in and destroying my life like the 'Lord of Death', in one sweep, that I was almost used to the carnage and destruction that she caused to my life. But on that final day I had had enough and walked away.

The first year was very difficult and I didn't know how I would get through it, so I did what I always do and worked and worked. This time something was changing for me because I couldn't keep it up. I didn't want to abuse myself as I had done in the past.

The overworking took its toll and I felt like I was living in hell. I noticed this very soon but I had taken on projects that I could not extricate myself from. I had to wait until the time was right.

I knew I had to move again and change my life drastically, otherwise what was the point of giving her up and giving up my life only to find myself in the same place. So I took a radical decision to sell up my house and give up work for a year, but that's another story and it is the reason I was now able to write this book.

I was in denial all my life about what my mother was really like, cruel. I hid that from myself in order to see her as a kind, lovely woman who loved me because owning up to the reality of who she was would have been too much. So I continued the facade as long as I could and became more and more depressed. When I realised what she truly was I left to save myself. The truth of that hurts, it will always hurt.

Are you prepared to say goodbye?

Contemplation

Going No Contact means that you will never see, speak to, contact or be part of your parent's lives. They are lost for ever to you and you have to let them, and the illusion that you created around them, go. Sit quietly and contemplate the enormity of this decision should you decide to take it. Some people choose to go 'Low Contact' maintaining some contact but limiting that. My parents were too destructive for me to go that route, it had to be final if I was to survive.

Don't underestimate the enormity of such a decision.

Before you go No Contact it may be worth writing down all the reasons why you may have difficulty making this drastic decision, so that you can re-read it should you be tempted to see her in a glowing light when you have gained some distance. Write down all the cruel things that you have experienced by her hands and ask yourself is this treatment normal for a mother?

- What support will you need when you go No Contact?
- If she looks for you how will you hide your trail?
- What are you prepared to give up to do this?
- Are you able to support yourself if you end up alone?
- Which coping device are you likely to use to numb the pain?

- What can you use to help you from not going back?
- Why did you decide to go NC?
- What will you gain if you stay?
- What will you gain if you go?
- What will you loose if you stay/go?
- Why do you think you mother has NPD?

When you decide to leave you will have to ask yourself what you will say if anything. Will you tell her you are going? Whatever you say you will get no closure. She may even try to manipulate you by being nice so that you will stay. Once you decide to go you have to make a commitment to stay away forever. If you go back things will only be worse. Think about the enormity of this decision.

From my own personal experience I can tell you that there is life after No Contact but it does take time to heal. I would never, ever, ever go back now, NEVER!

At first I questioned what I had done. Was I awful, cruel, unkind? That's how much they had trained me. Not any more.

You are not responsible for your mother though you will feel you are because that is what NPD does to a child. You are also not responsible for someone who had a responsibility for you and didn't look after you. You are however responsible for yourself and this is an enormous burden for many NPD survivors who have big empty holes where they were not parented with love, care and attention

I often wish I had someone to look after me, parent me but that will never happen. I have learned to parent myself and I am lucky to have the support of a man who I love and who loves me. Yet still some days I have a big gaping hole of not being nurtured. On those days I look after myself because I know what I need now.

If your mother had or has NPD you will never get from her the love you would like from her. It doesn't matter what you say or do she will never change. You, however, can change your life now that you realise what the problem is. You are innocent.

The next stage is grief as you begin to mourn her, your life and what you didn't have. You grieve for the lies you told yourself and the choices you made. Let's now look at how to grieve.

Tears in a dessert

Where am I to leave my tears?
There isn't a well big enough to contain,
the bitter tearful pain,
I could cry.
The rocks would be washed away to nothing,
if I start.
The crops ruined
and the lowlands flooded.
No one would survive from such a downpour,
certainly not I.
So I am left
unable to start,
like a battery run flat.
Trying to let go,
trying to release my pain,
to start the rain,
but it is a dessert plain
I own.

Alice Little

Grief

'The only real prison that exists is my own mind. If I conquer my mind I can conquer anything. The only jailer is myself and therefore I hold the key to my freedom.'
Alice Little

Perhaps the hardest part of letting go, going NC with one's parents is the aftermath of grief. It is like a funeral with no body, a funeral that one will not attend and no one may know about. This loss is enormous and I can't stress this enough. Not only because of the loss of physical and personal contact but also the loss of a world one had created and then come to know as a lie. That lie is a shock, shaking the core of your world and turning it upside down.

When you decide to go NC you also risk the loss of everything and everyone who held up and was part of the world that you inhabited while a member of that family of origin. Your losses can include your friends, siblings, family members, job, house, wealth, town and, most importantly, loss of self.

If you decide to go NC, your world as you knew it is broken and lost. For me there was no choice of shall I, shan't I. It happened and there was no other choice. If there had been I would have taken it. Although this may seem catastrophic, your life has fallen apart because it really wasn't together in the first place. This new life that takes its place is a coming together, rather than a falling apart. Think of it as 'the hero's journey' and 'the road less travelled'. Your story may be one that can never be told to another for the sheer reason that it is a secret. It may remain a secret because the sharing of it has to be done with thought. Others may be very judgemental of what you have done and, in the very beginning when you are at your most vulnerable, that can be hard to hear.

You may be in hiding because you know that your family will pursue you, not because they love you but because they have lost the victim that they need to play with and a scapegoat to project upon.

As with any broken relationships there can be an urge to want to go back, to relieve the pain, but, as with any addiction, the source has to be found and removed. You understand that you can not go back. What you had is not there any more. Once the veils are lifted from your eyes and the truth remains, you are awake and there is only a movement forward, never back.

If you should attempt to go back you will find that you have entered a town that was once home and you do not recognise it any more. You will talk to old friends and can not understand what they are talking about and they you. It is as if your life had vanished and now in its place is a sort of vapid illusion with blurred edges.

At this point you will enter a period of grief and letting go and it's never easy. Eventually you will come to a point of acceptance and be able to move on, with grief taking a back seat.

Never underestimate grief and think it's over with. Grief is something that acts beyond our understanding. It can creep up on you just when you have finished with it. Triggers to a place, a song, a memory can make it all flood back. When those times happen to me I look at it and ask myself "Am I indulging in this?". I also ask myself "Do I want to put myself through this by dwelling on it?". Sometimes I just cry and at those times the tears somehow seem different, more real, more healing.

Learning to grieve

Contemplation

Grieving for someone who has died goes through many stages. This process is the same for any form of loss, especially if the person is still alive but you have lost touch or have broken ties with them and Elizabeth Kubler-Ross, a specialist of grief and dying described these stages as;

- Denial
- Anger
- Bargaining
- Depression
- Acceptance

These stages are different for everyone and can happen in a different order and also be repeated. These stages are just a guide for you. Read these stages and find out if they apply to you and how to deal with each one. Maybe you will find some stages of your own.

Denial

Even after you go NC you will still have periods of denial. Denying that she/they abused you, thinking it's all your fault. Adult survivors of narcissistic abuse are past masters of this stage and can keep up the denial that their parents had NPD and also the denial of abuse they suffered most of their life. Moving on from this stage will be a big step and it is also possible that it will recur. I found this stage a difficult one as I was so programmed to thinking everything was my fault and my poor mother was suffering not me. Eventually it grows dimmer and you start to see her for what she was and what she did. You can no longer deny it and then you may move onto the next stage.

Anger

You may feel anger towards your parents and feel the injustice of having lived a lie. You will see how the abuse affected your life and your choices and the wasted opportunities you may have lost. It's OK to feel anger but acting on it never is. If your parents had NPD you will have seen how destructive anger is when acted upon in that moment when the emotion is at its highest. Anger will teach you a lot about your boundaries and how they have been stepped over. Before you react breathe and take a step back, chances are you will be more productive and have a better outcome if you do so.

Bargaining

We know this one very well. Pleading with parents to not hurt us and promising to do anything to keep them happy and wanting them to love us. You can not bargain with a narcissist as they have nothing to bargain with. If only you had loved them more - you loved them too much! At this stage you wonder if you could have done anything differently or said something differently. You would do anything to get the love back of your abusive cruel mother. Was it that bad? Isn't it worse now? Then you realise that you bargained all your life and nothing changed. Giving up that hope you may move onto the next stage, depression.

Depression

When you see the hopelessness of the situation and the truth that you can't go back and will never see them again you may fall into a depression. Everything can seem hopeless and you feel that you can't live without them. But you must get through this part by at least giving yourself the satisfaction of healing in order to win the battle that you have been staging with the narcissist. You must win, this will be your triumph. You will heal and thrive because they haven't managed to destroy you. You left to heal and give yourself a new life. You may feel depressed and why wouldn't you, you just lost the most important relationship of your life. This period of depression is part of your journey and when you come out from under that dark cloud you will start to see maybe there is a future. You begin again and realise that there is no going back.

Acceptance

When you get to this stage you realise the truth of your situation and it is time to move forward. Things can seem pretty dull at first as you have been living through so much drama and that in itself can be addictive. The pain of loosing her lessens and you are able to move on. It is a huge thing you have done to be courageous enough to go against her and leave. Your strength returns and you can eventually use your pain and suffering to inspire others. You begin to get ready for the world again and to heal enough to pass on any knowledge you may have gained. Your suffering has not been in vain if it can inspire another.

Looking at grief

Contemplation

Contemplate and write down each of the stages of grief and see how it has affected you. Do this process regularly and see where you are within the stages and what you need to support yourself through this most difficult time.

See if you can find any other stages that you have been through or are going through. How did you cope with this?

What would you say to the little child that lived through this? Tell her and promise that you will treat her from now on with respect.

Give yourself time to grieve you will learn from these times.

Because I love

Because I love,
the colours of my dreams are vibrant and alive.
My world is filled with a joy
that has no words.
I am in touch with the beloved,
in me and other.
Gone beyond self and turned
into an angelic being.
I will never give up on love,
because
the option is not open to me.
I have broken the shell that covered
my soft underbelly,
melted my frozen heart,
set me free.
Give, give, give,
then in the emptiness,
the eternal beating heart,
that is mine.

Alice Little

Spiritual emergency

'You can't get apples from planting a rice crop'
Sogyal Rinpoche

My world as I knew it fell apart and unravelled quite unexpectedly and suddenly. I started to have flashbacks to my childhood and I knew it was part of something much greater than myself. It was so all-consuming and indescribable that I only just managed to keep it together. It happened very suddenly and then became steadily intrusive until it took over my life. At the time I had no counselling or support system and what was happening to me had no name. I held on and trusted that what I was going through was a sort of waking up and allowed the process to happen.

When I first started to admit to the abuse of my childhood it was a very difficult time. Child abuse was not discussed, certainly not in the media and never in public. Any self help books I found had to be ordered from a secret bookseller online. Child abuse was shameful for a survivor and shameful to talk about, so you hid it.

The False Memory society were in full force, why wouldn't they be? The secrecy of their little paedophile paradise was in danger of being eroded. This society was created by paedos in America who owned a paedophile paper called Finger, says it all really! Also at that time the P.I.E "paedophile information exchange" was running and they were trying to lower the age of consent limit.

My flashbacks started one day when I admitted to my husband that I had been abused as a child by a family member and that very admission opened up a whole load of memories. Even as I said it, I said it without feeling, not even believing myself. I had never told a soul up to that point and I think admitting it was an opening my mind was looking for.

Everything that I remembered that only had a beginning and an end before now had a middle. Although it was very painful to

34

recollect and live through these events again, I felt that I was becoming whole in a strange way and my life, and how it had been up to now, made sense.

The memories came flooding back and could happen at any time, any place, as if it were happening now. I don't know how I managed to hold down a job or even function with others. It must have appeared strange to see from the outside, though mostly I put on a mask and kept it hidden, shame made sure of that.

As the memories surfaced I could no longer deny the abuse that had happened at my mother's hands when just a tiny child. The beatings were constant and the put-downs regular. People expect men to abuse but with women it's hidden very deeply under the guise of nurture and women can get away with abuse because no one believes that it's in their nature.

As both a child and an adult I had divided my mother into two people in order to cope, one was the good mother and the other mother did the abuse and was not my mother. This is a normal response to a situation in which a care-giver is abusing you. It meant that I could carry on seeing her as a good mother but the downside was that I blamed myself because if she was good then I must be bad.

I had to confront both my mother and father, it just wasn't an option to keep it hidden again, but the outcome wasn't pleasant. At first my mother pretended to be OK and we kept up some communication that led me to believe that everything was all right. I was pretending to myself again because one day, out of the blue, she decided she didn't want to see me again because of what I'd accused her of, and that she would never get over it. She didn't contact me again and ten years went by before I went looking for her and made contact with her myself.

For a brief time it was wonderful to think that I had her in my life again but it didn't take long to realise that she was playing games with me and using siblings to gang up against me. It never felt right with her because I was no longer under her spell and had changed a lot. She could put on a front but I could see behind it.

She tried to manipulate me and control me as before but this time I could see through it. Even so I still ignored many unkind things she did and tried to make excuses. She wasn't happy that I had boundaries, she hated that and tried to push them again and again. In the time after she had made the decision to cut me out of her life, when I had confronted her with her abuse of me, I had changed. She, however, had not changed at all.

So when we finally made contact again I was no longer prepared to let her treat me badly or to wait for the ambush she was setting up for me. I could see it clearly and so I took my exit and left her for the last time.

How has your life been up to now?

Contemplation

Take a good long look at yourself and see how your life story has shaped up. Ask yourself some deep questions about this. Here are a few to get you thinking, you can add your own later.

- Do you think you are not normal, mad or bad?
- Are you a carer putting others first?
- Are you afraid of your mother?
- Are you afraid of women/men?
- Do you push yourself too hard?
- What is your coping device?
- Do others take advantage of you?
- Do you say yes when you mean no?
- Do you say no when you mean yes?
- Are you secretive?
- Do you make friends easily?
- Are you a people pleaser?
- Do you have a lot of empathy for other's suffering?

Scapegoat

I am the family scapegoat.
I have been sent
out,
into the wilderness,
to fend for myself.
They have pinned on my coat,
all the things
in themselves,
that they detest.
Given to me to wear,
the blackest of sheep.
I thought at first
that these things pinned to me,
were mine,
that my soul
was black to the core.
But over time
I started to take them off,
one by one,
to become who I am today,
a sheep
with no coat
and no home.

Alice Little

Being in recovery

*'Because I have been moulded by so many for their own purpose
I have forgotten who I am, but I'm remembering, and it scares
them.'*
Alice Little

Say this to yourself, *'I'M IN RECOVERY'*. You may or may not
be addicted to a substance but you are addicted to her. This
realisation will give you a new found respect for those who are
actually addicted and/or recovering from their addiction.

There is something real about those who are addicted to alcohol
or drugs as it's very obvious they are in pain and it shows.
Whereas most people who consider themselves not addicted to
something, however trivial, can hide their sorrow in other ways
that are accepted by society (good luck with that one, its
exhausting!).

It's much easier but also just as painful, if not more so, to stay
latched on, hooked in and obedient to the mother with NPD. You
can decide to forgive her and everything will be all right for a
while until she injects you once again with her narcissistic poison.
With any poison you need to know the antidote and in this case it
is to go 'NO CONTACT'. To utterly go cold turkey and sit with
the withdrawal symptoms that you will feel when you decide to
cut her poison out of your life and become well in both body and
mind.

In my recovery I have days when I feel I can't cope. I wonder
about death and illness and other sorts of anxiety inducing
thoughts. The only thing that keeps me going is knowing that it
won't last, it's impermanent. Just as if it's a rainy day it won't last
and tomorrow it may be sunshine.

Anything can happen in life. You only have to trust that it really
is impermanent and see the truth of it in your own life. People go
from being poor to becoming rich and vice versa. A person who

has been a hardened criminal can turn their life around and work for the good of others.

Whatever you are going through right now, at this moment, just trust the process and what the future will hold for you and keep that glimmer of light in sight.

Some days I see people in the street that look like my mother and I can be swayed by memories of her. As time goes on, and this still happens, I can now choose whether I want to indulge in this or just see it as a thought and not follow it. Why would I want to hurt myself by indulging?

In order to recover you have to see what it is that you are addicted to, stop the source and start recovery. It may not be a linear process and you may falter and stumble, but having admitted that something is wrong is the first step.

From now on you will have to be honest with yourself and look at the reason why your life has been the way it was.

Writing your life story

Contemplation

Start by writing the story of your childhood and following it through to the present day. This story will help you to see the patterns that have been created and to which you unconsciously adhere to, bringing it into the present consciousness and healing it.

When you sit down to write your story it can be both a painful and liberating experience, therefore be gentle with yourself, take breaks. You will become exhausted if you try to do this in one sitting.

Just start with the earliest memory you have and ask yourself is this something that I remember or is it some event that my mother repeats over and over and so I think it's a memory?

Mothers with NPD want to re-write your childhood and leave out their abuse and give you a perfect childhood instead. My mother would always tell the same stories about my childhood again and again and they were always the same few.

When I recounted even simple things I remembered she had no recollection. I even went back to a place I lived to confirm that a certain landmark I remembered was there and was so excited to find that I hadn't made it up. When I told her she still doubted it was true.

You could begin just by journaling every day and saying how you feel, because if your mother has NPD there is a good chance that you don't know how to feel.

Inner child writing

You may also want to do some inner child writing to heal those parts of you that are wounded and affecting your present day. When you do inner child writing imagine that you are talking to your younger self. Be aware that this child is in pain and may not trust you to open up their dialogue. Keep at it and you will be in awe of what comes out of this process.

When I did inner child work I wasn't aware of what it was called, it just flowed. I accessed parts of myself that I had shut off and was able to integrate these lost parts into my being and started to feel whole again.

Many of these parts had names and personalities and modes of dress, not unlike multiple personalities, but they contained parts of my memory that were so painful that my mind had creatively contained them as if they were the memories of another. When I explored this in detail I would often find that I had contained the memories in personalities that resembled my abusers and I totally understood why this would happen to help me to deal with something too painful to withstand.

I was able to speak to those wounded parts of me buried so deep, so untrusting and damaged. I was able to integrate them within the empty shell of a being I had become and it was so healing. When you have a past that is empty and you hear others speak of their past in such detail you envy that. Then finally you realise that it was so awful and so traumatic why would you remember it.

It is difficult to believe in parts of yourself that are split off. You must be aware of them in order to heal them, those split off parts that were unable to speak up. No one would have believed them then but now you have a role to play as the one person who will now listen to and believe finally what that child went through.

I have also met people who have no memories but just know that they were abused. Those people found it very difficult to deal with just having a knowledge and feeling but no pictures. If you are one of those people just trust yourself, trust your inner self. You don't need pictures in your mind to acknowledge abuse. You can see by your life how bad your childhood was. Why would you make this stuff up? Why would you want to admit it and hurt yourself so much?

When you do this deep inner work make sure that you have time afterwards to rest as it can be emotionally draining. This work will eventually vitalise you as you wake up long forgotten parts of yourself and become whole again.

Mother

I love you so much
that I would be unable
to express
such a thing in words.
It is as if
I have torn out my heart
and given it to you.
Do you love me?
I ask again and again.
I long for your love,
long to be free of the pain
of unrequited love.
It is only your love
I want
but I can't have it.
So I am restless and wandering,
needy and abandoned.
Not fit to live among others
with this empty hollow
in which my heart lies.
You, should be in that place,
in my heart.
I love you too much.

Alice Little

Absent Mother/Invisible Father

'I have a deep, dark, huge hole in my centre that you took from me. I'm filling it up with the love you never gave me.'
Alice Little

I was well aware that my father was always absent. I just didn't realise how much it had affected me and that his absence was just a part of my life. Whereas my mother, who I thought of as perfect, was, in fact, even more absent than he was.

Both of them were absent when they weren't there and absent when they were. They were emotionally unavailable and later in my life I discovered that the problem with me was not that I was mad but that they were. Both of them had Narcissistic Personality Disorder (NPD).

How do I know this? Were they diagnosed? If you understand what a personality disorder is then you can understand that these people would never go for help or try to change themselves. That is because their personality disorder makes them think that there is nothing wrong with them.

I discovered this when I had gone NC with both my parents once again and this time for good. When looking on the internet to see if other daughters had problems with their mothers in the same way as myself.

I came across several sites about survivors of NPD abuse. What I read shocked me and yet made absolute sense and at that time I started to wake up from the lies and the made up world their madness had taken me into.

I knew then that this wasn't just a parting of the ways that could be taken up again some time in the future. What I read made me realise how sick both my parents were and I knew then that I would never see them again.

Even though I take full responsibility for my own personal growth, still I find that the legacy they left me creeps up and enters my world and all I can do is learn how to live with it. I don't expect an end result, just to walk a different path to that which they led me along.

They are still affecting my life. No matter how much distance I place between myself and them, this deep scar of wounding opens up again, this wounding that feels as if they had placed it inside of me, is never completely healed. Yet there are days of which I feel are mine. The other days feel as if they are stolen from me and I want those days back.

Trying to purge these people from my life has been a long and tiring road. I decided enough was enough and now have chosen to live beyond the trauma of early years and to discover who I am and see something positive emerge from the events, how it has made me who I am and how to be OK with that.

I'm learning to live again. It is as if I have given birth to myself and I don't know who I am, its all new. I have no manual for this and at times I admit to feeling scared or overwhelmed. Yet I carry on as I always have done waiting for my life to begin. They took my life from me and I have to fill that place, that space they left within me. Sometimes it's a hard and lonely road and its easy to forget I am free at last. One gets used to chains.

Learning to parent yourself.

Contemplation

When your parents haven't nurtured you there can be a deep hole within. This need can manifest in a constant searching for either a person or an idea which can fulfil this need. You can only fill this need yourself and looking for it outside can lead to further abuse. Narcissists love needy people. You will have to find a way to nurture yourself which is something you may also have neglected up until now.

Ask yourself:
- In what way do I not care for myself?
- Is there anything I can do right now to nourish myself in both body and mind?
- Do I eat healthily?
- Do I over eat?
- Do I get enough exercise?
- Do I exercise too much?
- How can I have fun?
- Do I have friends that support me?
- Are my thoughts positive?
- Do I look after my environment?

Visualisation

Imagine a world for yourself that is free from her abuse. Include anything that she may have disapproved of or stopped you from doing. Create as much detail as possible. Make a mood board with pictures of what you would like in your life. When you have finished make some notes about what you visualised and see if you can make any of them come true. Create for yourself the life you now deserve.

Thickets

I have been into the darkest,
deepest woods,
where there is
no light,
no life,
no hope.
Thickets and brambles
have scratched my
sensitive skin.
Blinded by darkness,
so thick
I could hold it.
I had to do this,
to go within.

Alice Little

Coping Device

*'Relaxation is not something that comes easy to me, some effort
has to be made. If I put as much effort into relaxing as I do in
being hyper-vigilant, by now it would have become a good habit.'*
Alice Little

I didn't realise that I had been living a lie but deep inside and
probably visible on the outside to others, I felt a fraud,
uncomfortable in my own skin. People can often sense that and it
looks weird. I think that if I admit it I am slightly Autistic and I
definitely put that down to my childhood trauma.

Holding it all together by the skin of my teeth, I managed to live
what could be seen as a normal and even a successful life. But it
had to end, had to fall apart. The house that I had built on sinking
sand with no foundations and no support.

This holding together was in fact very unhealthy, physically and
especially mentally. There was only one coping device I knew
that would block out my pain and hide the truth from myself and
that thing was work.

My coping device was to work hard. It was my addiction and
my refuge. It could easily have been drink, gambling, drugs or sex
but somehow none of those took a hold or came into my view. All
of these things that I could have been addicted to, I see now, had
passed so near to me in my life yet had been too invisible to take
a hold.

When I was given the opportunity to work at my first job it was
a fix like no other. It became my friend and my support and a
place to hide in as well as to shine. Here was something that I was
good at. The input of negative comments that I had been taught
were not applying here. I was being told that I was good at
something and I gave 101% back in the form of being the most
perfect and interested apprentice.

My early education had been mediocre. I had a few good
teachers and I was grateful for their input but my infant school
teachers were often bullies. My parent's divorce changed the

whole course of my education in that I either did much better than expected for my age or I did really badly depending on how things were at home. My parents didn't help me with any school work or encourage me to learn or look at my future. I wasn't expected as a girl from a poor background to make anything of myself. A career was not what I was educated for yet when I left school with no exam results I was told I would amount to nothing. They were wrong. I had a long and successful career.

Until I was given my first pay rise I had been handing over all of my money to my stepmother. Once I got a pay rise I gained new found financial freedom and strength and could see some independence arising from this. Within three years from that date I would have moved out from that unhappy home for good and into a shared flat.

I felt that I was being paid for a hobby and I loved the creative aspect and freedom of expression that the job gave me. As time went on the nature of the job began to change and the hours I worked grew longer. I was often working outside of 9-5 hours, sometimes late into the night and even early into the next morning and even weekends.

The problem was that I didn't know when to stop, in fact I couldn't stop. I didn't know that the busyness was to stop me from seeing how much in pain I was and if I stopped I may have seen that.

Within two years of starting work I was so bad with my nerves, due to not only my mother, but now my unkind and cruel stepmother, that my doctor put me on anti-depressants and asked me if I wanted to involve social workers. I said no because I was afraid and didn't really know what that meant.

If the doctor had explained that to me I may have gone down a different route, perhaps for the worse for I'm sure I may have ended up in care. In those days the parents were rarely at fault and I would surely have been looked at as a difficult child.

I didn't know then that I had Post Traumatic Stress Disorder, no one saw it or cared. I cried endlessly and was very depressed. Something inside me has always kept me going and driving me but that driven side took over and I let it and my body paid the price.

Your coping devices

Contemplation

- What coping devices did you use as a child to deal with your pain?
- What do you do now to overcome your anxiety?
- Could you give up your coping device if it is dangerous for you?
- Could you modify the behaviours you have learned in order to cope?
- Did you gain anything from your abusive childhood?
- In what way can you turn anything negative in your life into a positive outcome?
- What would be the outcome if you give up your coping devices?
- What would be the outcome if you keep your coping devices?

Shoes

Why must they always better me,
be one step ahead of
my shoes,
which are well worn,
from walking behind them,
never with them.
My sock-less feet are cold,
waiting for their glances
to warm me,
warm my feet,
touch my feet
with their hands
and show me
their mercy.
Why must they be above me?
Why can't they love me?
Never near
or next
or beside.
Their pride
or mine
keeps them from slipping on my shoes
and I theirs.

Alice Little

Habits

'If you do it more than once it's a habit'
Sogyal Rinpoche

Our habits are very quickly entrenched. One only has to do something twice in order for it to become habitual and get a hold on us. You only have to re-arrange the inside of your cupboards to find out your habits as you will still find yourself looking in the same cupboard for something that has now been moved.

It is also the same with the way we think, it becomes so habitual that we think our thoughts are us and we take them far too seriously. We then find it hard to give up thoughts that are habitual because we feel that we would be giving up ourselves.

It's a difficult thing to do, giving up our habits. We become so comfortable with them that it's like putting on an old pair of slippers, when they wear out its difficult to replace them. New slippers feel tight and uncomfortable.

As a child we are open and like a sponge to the ideas and thoughts of adults, learning from them the behaviours they want from us in order to make life better for them. If the adult who guides us is incapable of seeing and being aware that in front of them is an undeveloped child and not an adult, how different would the interaction be.

If a child is brought up by a parent who has NPD then the child becomes an extension of the parent rather than flourishing as an individual. The parent sees the child as a mirror of themselves and if the child does not live up to this idealised image, which is impossible, the child learns to adapt and acquiesce and loses its sense of self.

This adapted child can later on become depressed and anxious and will not know the reason they feel this way because they can't see that the parent has created this problem.

This happened to me and I learned to adapt and be good to a certain extent but I was never able to live up to my parent's idea of who I should be. It was as if I had been brought by a stork into the wrong family and all they could see was an ugly duckling and all I could see was an ugly duckling.

Even so there was always something in me which was slightly rebellious and once I left school and began work that kicked in a bit more. I had a bit of a defiant attitude which sometimes I kept hidden from them but sometimes it came out. As I got older this turned into the protection mode of what appeared like arrogance (I'm still arrogant!) which covered my soft heart and vulnerability. My heart is something they were unable to take from me, no matter how badly they treated me they were unable to destroy my goodness. That was mine and remains so.

Finding your habits

Contemplation

There are good habits and bad habits. You can tell if they are bad habits by how much they are damaging you and making you unhappy. Good habits however are harder to learn, bad habits are easy but in the end more painful. If you attach the thought of excruciating pain to your bad habits and massive joy to your good habits when they occur, you may be able to turn them around.

Begin by becoming aware of habits that have become normal for you and write them down. Next to each one on the list write the outcome if you continue to indulge in them. In another line next to that write the positive outcome if you give up these habits.

Keep going back to this list whenever you are tempted to habitually do something damaging and look at what the outcome will be if you continue. Keep a chart of your success and what stopped you from succeeding if you didn't. Don't expect to change overnight as your habits will have been laid down for many years.

If I became very bored with my habits and was totally disinterested in them as if they were a bad friend, I ceasing to make them VIPs in my mind.

Myself exposed

If you read my poetry
you will know
that I was a woman
who struggled
with life,
lived with pain.
You will know me
deeply,
from my words.
I was not a shallow woman
and for that
I have no regrets.
Because I lived
deeply
outside the every day boundaries
of a shallow world.
I swam against the tide
created my own wake
leaving behind,
memories,
for you.

Alice Little

Guilt

'Guilt is for picture frames'
Sogyal Rinpoche

When you have been trained by a narcissist from birth you will have guilt in bucket loads. In fact you will feel guilty about being guilty.

Going NC is bound to bring out feelings of guilt. You have left her and she had primed you to care about her and not yourself. You may be called selfish by her and others and you already feel selfish by walking away. Remember that it is her that is selfish because if she wasn't you would be able to talk this out like adults and move on. Instead you are faced with a two year old toddler who may rant and rave at you and make no sense.

She trained you to never abandon her no matter how harsh the treatment, however she can and will and probably has abandoned you. She can do this because she knows that she can do anything to you and you will always forgive and go back to her. You may even plead with her to come back.

The guilt of being a bad person is the problem, aren't you supposed to be good and if you became a bad child well that's what she would expect from you anyway. You are now going to be going against all that she taught you and when you were a child there were repercussions to such an action. There will be repercussions now too but as an adult this will be repaid in a different way. She may turn your friends, spouse and employees against you. She may blacken your name in the town you live in, she will want to get you back for what you have done to her.

She will lie to you and even be nice to you, but it will not last. She will use phrases to hook you in emotionally, she may cry and even use illness or old age to coerce you. You are primed to skip to her tune and you must learn to block out that tune.

In order to gain freedom you have to sever the ties that bind you to her, not be afraid of her wrath and escape. She will come after you but don't be mislead, she doesn't love you she just wants to wreak revenge. She may even try to use your children against you, keep them safe and don't let them go through the same childhood as you.

Eventually you will stop feeling guilty and will see how this kept you tied to her. Once you have had space from her for a period of time instead of guilt you will have time to look after yourself and take away the neediness she used to suck you dry and instead learn to nurture and love yourself again.

What makes you feel guilty?

Contemplation

When we are children we long for our parent's love and approval. We are rewarded for so called good behaviour and punished for bad behaviour. As adults we carry this conditioned guilt which stops us from behaving in ways which we think others will not approve of. It can turn us into people pleaser's and make us be incapable of being who we really are. We learn to adapt our behaviours in order to be liked. If we say or do something we think others will not approve of, then we feel guilty.

- What makes you feel guilty?
- Does your guilt belong to now or the past?
- What behaviours were you rewarded for as a child?
- What behaviours were you scolded for?
- In what way can you learn to feel innocent instead of guilty?

On a blank sheet of paper write down the affirmation as many times as you like:
' I am innocent'
' I am innocent'
' I am innocent'

Love

Love doesn't die
It is eternal
It flows like a stream
From a vast well
that has no end
It is all pervasive
Sometimes hidden
Never give up
on love

Alice Little

Siblings or friends

'They kept us apart, it's called divide and rule. I saw that and escaped.'
Alice Little

When you have grown up in a family where a parent or parents have NPD, your relationship with your siblings will have been destroyed. NPD parents create disorder by having favourites. Because parents with NPD have no other interest but themselves they get their children to fight with each other for their attention.

If you have escaped chances are that you were the black sheep and the scapegoat of the family, wearing all the disowned parts of everyone. There will have been a sibling who was the 'Golden Child' and could do no wrong and if there are other siblings they may be the 'Lost Child' who is ignored.

The parent can switch these roles between each sibling but the main effect is to keep you apart and to vie for the crumbs of love you long for but never receive.

In my family I was definitely the black sheep and never fitted in and could do nothing right to please them. Whereas my brothers were golden mummy's boys who seemed to receive much more than I ever did.

When I went NC with my parents I continued to be in contact with my brother who I later realised was just a mule for them. It took a while to realise that his only interest in me was to take back information to them. My other brother ended up living near my mother and wouldn't speak to me. I eventually went NC with them all and it was a huge relief to end it all even though painful.

I wondered why there was a strangeness between us, as if there was a barrier. I was jealous of my parent's affection and attention to my siblings because I was being ignored or abused. I see now that my siblings also had a bad time but that it is not my responsibility. They remain within the family and I remain outside rejected by them all unless I get back into my role.

How can we be expected to communicate effectively with others when our own family of origin is split from the very beginning. In an ideal world families would bring up children as future citizens and make sure that they were going to be a valuable member of society.

Unfortunately family problems are trans- generational and secret and talking about one's family being dysfunctional is avoided. We all live in a world of lies where we pretend that we are having a good life when we are not. When you step off the treadmill of doing this you wake up and see things as they truly are. Life is not necessarily any easier but you are no longer fooled by anyone.

The same thing that Narcissists do to siblings is the same thing they will do to you and your friends.

Your place within the family

Contemplation

In a family that is not dysfunctional children will grow within that unit, working out their place within it and growing healthily. They will be able to move into the adult world with a knowledge of how people interact healthily. In a dysfunctional family you are given a place to be that keeps you away from your siblings while keeping you in your place. When you move into the adult world you are ill equipped to survive in a way that would be beneficial for you or others. Especially so if you have been the scapegoat of the family. Taught to wear that label within the family you think it is normal and so enter an adult world thinking that this is your role.

- Can you remember how your parents treated your siblings/friends?
- In what way was it different to your treatment?
- Do you get on with your siblings?
- What were your siblings rewarded for?
- Can you see your position within the family?
- If you didn't have siblings how did they treat your friends compared to you?

Autumn walk

Browned, crunched, scrunched,
like burnt paper
Underfoot on green carpets,
the Autumn,
the end of Summer.
Each day
breeze
upon skin.
Wet winds, wet hair and wet eyes.
Silence where once noise and play
Now the crowds have gone home.
Solitary figures,
hunched in wooden seats
that bear the names of the dead.
Oak trees that have seen many lives.
Now that dying time of year
extends it's long fingers.
I love the peace of this time.
No summer missed by me.
Just cool days,
just time,
just lovely.
Scrunch and crunch of leaves
on green carpets.

Alice Little

The sensitive personality

*'I have more respect for a man who lets me know where he
stands, even if he is wrong.
Than one who comes up like an angel and is nothing but a devil'
Malcolm X*

If you have grown up with parents who have NPD the chances are
that you have a sensitive personality. Because you were always on
alert and trying to please parents who can not be pleased, you
would have spent your time trying to define everything from how
they were feeling, looking and acting and never wondering how
you felt.

As an adult you will carry on this sensitivity and somehow feel
uncomfortable with it. It is likely that if you are a sensitive person
that narcissists will be attracted to you and you to them.

This cycle has to be broken in order to stop further abuse. You
will find your own way to deal with this. For me I kept myself
alone and safe for years watching and waiting and learning, just
like I did when I was an apprentice as a young girl.

I am re-learning all that I was taught and filling it in with some
good honest facts of life. My narcissist detector is becoming a
finely tuned radar. After all, her abuse gave me a better than most
sensitivity to people, atmospheres and places, so it is this skill that
I now use for my benefit.

Make no mistake these narcissists are slippery characters and
can easily fool you. The most important thing that I have learned
is that you have to work out where you are the most needy, the
place that is empty and needs filling.

If you don't know where your neediness is then along will come
the narcissist with the exact thing you lack and give it to you. If
you succumb you will become under their spell and once hooked
it is much harder to escape.

Once you admit your needs and are able to address those needs
yourself the narcissist will no longer be interested in you and you
will not be looking for them to fill you up.

Coming to terms with the fact that you are a sensitive person will give you confidence and self- acceptance.

Personality traits

Contemplation

Here is a list of personality traits that you may have if you are a sensitive person due to having parents with NPD. It is not definitive and you may resonate with some or even add your own. The list is to give you a wake up and a nudge, because if you identify with a lot of them you may realise you are not alone in who you are, that there are other marvellous souls just like yourself. This contemplation is slightly longer because it is something that you will find can be a positive outcome of your experience with NPD parents.

- Kind
- Easy going
- Attract loud, bossy people
- People pleaser
- Struggle with intimacy
- Being too intimate too quickly
- Sensitive to other's needs
- Ignoring your own needs
- Sensitive to your environment
- Ability to read others immediately
- Not fooled by other's masks
- Wanting to help others
- Getting over involved in other's problems
- Ignoring your needs
- Spiritual seeker

- Inability to be around angry people
- Abhorrence of any form of cruelty
- Aversion to violent, horror films
- Quiet
- Preferring solitude
- Feeling not understood
- Always on the outside
- Not fitting into groups
- Thinking your mad
- Thinking everyone else is sane
- Moving home frequently
- Wanting to leave soon after you arrive somewhere
- Anxiety
- Easily stressed
- Artistic
- Imaginative
- Creative
- Sensitivity to light
- Sensitivity to flashing images
- Sensitive to sound
- Secretive

This list of traits is endless and from the ones listed here several will resonate plus you may have a few of your own. This list at first can seem negative, but in who's eyes? Do you identify with any? Add a few of your own.

Changing your perception

Contemplation

Look once again at the list above plus adding your own traits but now start to look at the list as if these traits were normal and accepted. Swap round the idea that any of them are not normal and you will find the truth of who you really are. The problem lies not with your self but other's perception of you. In a world where loud and aggressive personalities are rewarded you can find no space in this world for yourself. But every dog has its day and soon the time for sensitive and intuitive people will come.

So here is the list again with a different slant. It's just my interpretation and you can do this for yourself to suit your distinct and individual personality.

- I am nourished by my kindness
- My easy going nature is calming to others
- Loud and bossy people are not my real friends
- I have been taught to please others first and this makes me conducive to another's suffering
- I am sensitive to my environment which helps me to avoid danger
- Being able to read others helps me to not waste time.
- Not being fooled by other's masks makes me empathetic to their suffering
- Wanting to help others means I have a heart
- Because I am prone to get over involved in other's problems I stay aware and focused
- I can ignore my own needs and so I create a space to listen to what I do need.
- I'm a spiritual seeker and therefore have a great depth to my life

- Anger hurts everyone it touches and I prefer not to be around it
- Cruelty is a projection of self hatred, I choose kindness
- I watch my mind and everything I put into it
- When quiet I have space to see things clearly
- Solitude is a great gift
- Not being understood by others does not define me.
- Because I am often on the outside I get a clearer picture of what is happening on the inside.
- A group that is worth joining will include me
- Great yogis of the past often appeared to be mad
- With my intuition I see that everyone suffers mentally
- My real home is within me and can be found
- I can sit with the feeling of fear while longing to leave.
- My anxiety is a sign that my nervous system is overworked
- Because I know I am easily stressed I can avoid situations if I wish
- Being artistic is a great gift
- I use my imagination to create beauty
- My creativity helps me to move around situations
- My sensitivity to light allows me to avoid supermarkets!
- My sensitivity to flashing images helps me to avoid being hypnotised
- I am secretive and therefore can keep a secret

Letter to myself

If I could go back
and tell her just once,
that I loved her,
that I felt for her,
that I admired her
I would.
Can I do it now?
Can I stop, talking to her like her parents did?
Can I stop judging her, pushing her?
What if I asked her,
what do you want to do?
Instead of telling her.
What would she say?
She looks lonely,
perhaps she needs……
What do I know what she needs.
No one ever asked her,
or cared.
I'm trying to care for her now.

Alice Little

Living for myself

'Nobody can give you freedom, nobody can give you equality or justice or anything.
If your a man you take it'.
Malcolm X

I used to live my life for my mother. It sounds strange but every experience I had I lived it for her. I didn't know where she began and I left off. When I had good experiences I offered them to her in my mind, brought her to the event and gave it to her, denying myself the feeling of it all.

I didn't realise that I was doing this, I thought it was normal but when I did realise I found out how un-lived my life had been. I saw how good things in my life had passed me by as if they hadn't happened to me. I had just been an observer. In the eyes of the narcissist you do not exist, you only exist as an extension of them and this is how I became.

Now that I have let her go I have to take the courage to start to live and experience life and it's very scary because it's a new experience. Life remains at times dulled at the edges, devoid of feeling.

My whole life had been lived in a cloud of depression, numbed from life I was half dead, peering from behind her skirts at life, even as an adult. Now that the depression has lifted I find myself in a strange new land that I know nothing about and am afraid to try. My depression kept me more and more isolated and shut off from joy.

What does it feel like to really live fully? I don't mean to do daring, dangerous things as that in itself can also come from not feeling fully and creating adrenaline rushes so you can feel more. I mean to really embrace life in all its aspects and take a chance that it may hurt. Joy is more scary, for being happy meant I would be slapped or made to be quiet and keep still.

I no longer live for her but instead tread slowly into a new world of living for myself. It feels naked and exposed and I don't feel that I have the skills sometimes.

It is a fast world that can not wait for those like myself who can be too slow to say, 'Yes I will come', 'Yes I'd love to talk to you', 'Join a club', 'Go for a walk with you'.

Some days I have the courage and some days I don't, mainly because I sense that people don't understand me. She has scrambled my brain and my interactions so that I falter easily. Yet I feel I have a lot to offer others, it's just that they pass me by and I them and we miss out on each other.

She didn't like me to have friends, it had to be her as the centre of attention always as it is with narcissists. So you never get a chance to shine or stand out, always behind someone, always in a supporting role, like she taught me to be.

But I am stubborn and there is a part of me she couldn't destroy or change and I don't know what it is but she wanted it and I didn't let her take it. I try to find what this is so that I can grow it and gain strength from it. I feel it but don't know what it is. All I know is that there is only me in here now, inside this body and mind and she has no place and no right to take any more of my life.

Finding out who you are

Contemplation

Because you had no sense of yourself other than the self your mother gave you, you may struggle to find what it is that you like to do or even think. You have lived your life through her eyes and what she wanted you to be. Finding a life beyond her will be your challenge. When the time is right you will find your own way in life and your own tribe (family). Don't rush to replace her until you are aware of what a narcissist appears like, because you don't want to replace her with yet another narcissist.

- In what way do you avoid living your own life?
- Do you find yourself living through other's lives?
- What can you do to explore new avenues?
- Could you try something you haven't tried before?
- Do you have a longing to do something that she would not have approved of?
- What exactly is stopping you from living fully?
- You have gone No Contact, is she still in your mind?

71

Funeral Rites

No one to mourn me when I die
No tears at my funeral
No relatives at my death bed
No celebration of my life past
No one to talk of my accomplishments
Or to go through my possessions left
No kind words to be uttered over my coffin
No one to buy a gravestone
With words that mark who I was
No one to pray for me after
To send off my soul for re-birth
Alone in life
alone in death
Nothing ever changed

Alice Little

Without her

'You have to live a life to understand it, tourists just pass through'.
Prince

As the days go by and time creates a longer distance between myself and the woman who was and is my mother, it becomes more bearable. The longing to be with her born of the huge hole that is the longing for the love and mothering she couldn't give, is now being filled with love of myself and self-nurturing.

Her face once so bright and sharp in my mind has dulled, as if an old photograph. I have to learn to mother myself now, something I had to do as a child but the strain was too great. If I don't mother myself I bear witness to her legacy and only bring abuse on myself. The self-hatred she taught me has to be eradicated if I am able to survive and go beyond just surviving.

I step away from that life and now must not look back. I have looked back and even tried to go back, but she wasn't as I remembered or had created. All that was left was the glaringly bad mother I had hidden so long ago, only now that she couldn't hit me she had to find other devious ways to hurt me and this time I wasn't going to stand for it. I walked away, without dialogue, knowing that there would be no happy ending.

The charade that we had both been a part of fell away and I could finally see what she was doing to me. In 'Transactional Analysis' it is said that you can't have a game without a racket, so I took away the racket and stopped playing the game.

For her I was no longer that pliant child or adult. Instead I was the stubborn defiant child she thought she had eradicated and beaten from me.

My life without her brings sanity and I choose sanity. The madness I felt when with her or even when away from her was only her own madness projected upon me, I just didn't know that. I wore her madness for her like a horsehair coat.

When I look back at her and how she was in the past I see how her madness exposed itself and I also see how I am becoming free of that stigma. The damage she has done has a line drawn under it, she can only hurt me if I let her and as she is no longer in my life I must make sure that the ghost of her handiwork is also exorcised.

I will always mourn for her, but now not at the expense of my health and well being. Sometimes outsiders can be more of a family than our blood relatives. Daughters of NPD mothers should exercise caution in who they choose as friends and not just dash into the arms of another who will fill their needs and use them.

Letting go of the Narcissist

Contemplation

When we are free of the narcissist no matter how distant it can still feel as if we are somehow attached. As if there were an invisible chord that was feeding them and draining us. This visualisation is very helpful in cutting those chords and can be done again and again.

Visualisation

Close your eyes and visualise grey chords of fine opaqueness attached to your body and going from you to the other person. This chord may be thick or thin and there may be several. Invoke in front of you whatever and whoever you think of as a spiritual helper. This can just be a form of bright light, or your higher self.

In your mind take a pair of scissors, knife, scythe, saw or a chopper or sword depending on how thick it is and cut the chord from your body at its source, releasing it and sending it up to the sun giving it another source of light to feed off and freeing yourself. Cut off any stray pieces and where the chord was, rub it with white light and heal it, closing it off from the narcissists source for good. Repeat as often as you need to.

Narcs

The narcissists come to my door.
Chewing my bones, sucking my blood, sticking their drip feeds
into my heart.
Cold as ice they stare but do not look.
Frozen from looks and books.
Stiff and unyielding from problem childhoods.
Trying to take my vital energy.
Fools and idiots thinking I believe their silly talk.
Thinking I don't see
their manipulative minds at work.
Quieter than a stealth bomber and equally as evil.
But I have armour, I was trained by an expert.
They fear my goodness, shield from my light.
I am the winner,
they loose not to know me.

Alice Little

Recognising the Narcissist

'I didn't see you at first, I was drawn like a moth to a dangerous hot light.
Now I see you and I fly above the light.'
Alice Little

Once you have removed yourself from the narcissist (your mother) you have to make a pact with yourself to both recognise a narcissist when you meet one and also a pact with yourself to learn how not to attract them in the first place.

It is not always easy to spot a narcissist, they can sweep you off your feet very quickly, especially if you are needy. Your neediness will come from lack of parental affection, attention and nurturing. The narcissist brings promise of being able to fill this giant lack, at first, after they have caught and trapped you, you will be filling their needs and lacks and it is a bottomless pit.

The narcissist, whether man or woman, has a vast, cold, empty heart devoid of empathy. They can emulate care and love and attention, but it's not real, it only serves to enslave you.

I am not an expert and can only speak from my own experience so can tell you that there are two kinds of narcissist. One will sweep you off your feet and promise you the earth and they may be very attractive with a beguiling personality. The other is very still, cold and unresponsive. They both have in common one thing; they don't love you, don't care about you and are as near to robots as you can get.

The narcissist can also be put into two camps, one will play a very long game and wait for you to succumb and the other will catch you off guard very quickly. I have one word of advice when you meet them run, run, run and don't look back.

Your stumbling block to warding off the narcissist will be your inability to not being nice and being too polite. Not wanting to hurt anyone's feelings you will be fair game, like a horse with sores on its back. As they have no interest in your feelings you will be loosing nothing by ignoring them. Be warned, they are very obsessive and persistent!

When it's over, which will usually be at their instigation, they will move on at lightning speed to the next victim. Your job is not to be a victim in the first place, it could cost you your life.

We all have some traits of narcissism but those with NPD are high on the spectrum and it's not until adulthood that these traits are recognised. It's highly unlikely that a narcissist will seek help.

You may ask yourself the question, "Am I a narcissist?" Would you be working on yourself if you were? You would never ask yourself that question in the first place.

Recognising the Narcissist

When I first left my narcissistic family I was surprised to find that nearly everyone I came into contact with seemed to be a narcissist. It seemed that having escaped I was now being thrown some more at me just to test me. This time I could actually see them and that is why I seemed to feel that everyone was a narcissist. I had woken up to narcissism big time and I could see them. Yet still there was work to be done, still a few got under my narc radar and fooled me. I was in a bad state of course, I was grieving, my world had fallen apart, again and therefore I was very vulnerable and needy. This first phase after No Contact was a big wake up to life. I took off my rose coloured glasses and stepped into the real world.

Check list

Here are just a few checks to help you to spot a narcissist, You may well be able to add to this list.

- **Grandiosity.** Thinking they are better than anyone else.
- **Entitlement and impatience.** Me first, what I need I get, now!
- **Lack of empathy.** They don't care about anyone and can't identify with other's feelings.
- **Attention seeking.** Like to be noticed, hate to be outshone.
- **Sex.** Addicted to it and can be alluring and charming
- **Its all about you.** Only if they want something
- **Its all about them.** Pay attention at all times
- **Leaders.** Not always because they are good at it but because they want to be boss, including of you.
- **Storytellers.** Lots of stories, many untrue, to inflate themselves
- **Sad stories.** To get you hooked.
- **Appearance.** They have to look good,
- **Criticism.** They can't take it but can dish it out.
- **Trail of bad relationships.** You're next.
- **Cheaters.** They can't help it they need attention
- **Defensive.** You're against them if you don't agree.
- **Incurable.** They can't be helped because they believe it's you.
- **Snobs.** Disdainful and patronizing.
- **Fantasist.** About success, power, beauty and brilliance.
- **Exploitative.** Takes advantage to achieve their own ends.
- **Envious.** Envious of others and thinks others are envious of them.

Deflecting the Narcissists

Contemplation

Now that you have some knowledge of NPD you will need to start recognising the narcissists you meet. Begin by seeing the narcissists you have already met and start to look out for warning signs. The narcissist can sweep you off your feet if you let them but now you are awake you can walk away from them and never look back. You know their game and decide to not play.

Sit quietly and remember all the suffering that you have been subject to at the hands of narcissists and write them and the person's name on separate pieces of paper. When you have finished, in a safe place burn them and watch the smoke of your past disappear and rejoice by dancing to inspiring music.

Stealer

It's always about you, isn't it?
About my loss of you,
my love for you,
the big huge hole that you made within me.
It was always about you,
no room for me,
you took me away and instead made me you.
Filtered life through your eyes,
to feel life through your feelings
and live my life,
for you.
So now that I am without you,
I am dead somewhere.
Dead in my head,
because
you stole me.

Alice Little

Healing

'There is no better than adversity. Every defeat, every heartbreak, every loss, contains its own seeds, its own lesson on how to improve your performance the next time'
Malcolm X

There are days when I am unable to fully participate in life. Being in crowds of people or just going out can feel overwhelming. But now I honour those days instead of ignoring them and pushing through them. There is an aura about those days when I know how I will be amongst others. My interactions will be more difficult and my speech stilted and awkward as if dumb.

A lot of this is due to Post Traumatic Stress Syndrome and also something which I have recently discovered I have, Temporal Lobe Epilepsy (TLE). I was shocked to find out that my increasing deja vu episodes were down to TLE amongst other symptoms.

The TLE has calmed now that I am more relaxed and less stressed. Many things contributed to my TLE including my mother's hand that frequently met with the side of my head plus, later in life, an accident when a heavy wooden slab fell and hit me on the side of my head and the mistake of visiting a chiropractor, who, after seeing him I had a 24 hour episode of Deja Vu and episodes for months after. Also a terrible early childhood environment living with dripping damp and black mould which I believe can all contribute to TLE.

I try to live within the boundaries of my condition without making it disable me and most days I can feel normal. My body, which can hurt all over, sometimes is pain free. Anxiety tenses me up and if I look closely at the pain I can see how it arrived that way.

My social anxiety which makes it difficult to meet or interact with people is something which I believe has got worse since I went 'No Contact" however I don't believe it will always be like that and I allow myself to heal before the day when I will meet my tribe so to speak. From the outside you would just see a lady going about her life and be unaware of the war zone that my childhood was and my adult life is.

Because my mother taught me that my needs were not important it is a learning curve to look after myself in a new way or to allow myself to do something for myself which can feel very selfish.

Life goes on without her and instead of just surviving I intend to be thriving.

Healing yourself – the journey

Contemplation

What can you do to aid your healing?
Make a list and refer to it.

Do you actually want to be whole and healed?
What stops you from feeling good?
What conditions has your childhood created and how can you help alleviate this?
Do you have a support network?
How do you look after your body?
How do you look after your mind?
How do you look after your spiritual life?
How do you look after your environment?

This House

This house is my home
It nurtures and supports me.
Yet even so,
having found a womb such as this,
I am still unattached,
still a wanderer.
Creating a womb for the next bearer,
of this fine abode.
Someone somewhere is waiting
to live here,
In the home I have loved to life

Alice Little

Starting again

*'My life ended where you left me, my life begins where I picked
myself up from that place'.*
Alice Little

In my life I have had many new beginnings, where everything I
have known has been taken and I have had to begin again. It
usually happens because what is falling apart was not right and
space has to be made so that something better can take its place. If
everything stayed the same there would be no growth.

When things fall apart it is a painful time and sometimes to
avoid the pain, a longing can come that makes you want to go
back, go back to the good old bad days! There is no going back
because what you had is gone, you will not find it again.

So you start again a bit weary and tired and longing for the
comfort of what is familiar. Slowly you realise that you are free
and you don't know what to do with your freedom, having been a
prisoner for so long. The courage is to step out of the prison and
never go back, instead see what is in front of you, a new life, a
better life, and embrace it.

When you start over again from having gone No Contact with
your mother the pull of her may overwhelm you. She trained you
from an early age to care for her rather than her caring for you.
Through time you will find this less and less. It may sound like a
platitude but time will heal more than anything, you have to be
patient.

The only way out of this is to act like you are a recovering
addict, she is your addiction and how she created who you are is
the problem.

Do you have the courage to change those habits and to
disbelieve all the negative things you think about yourself?
I would love to tell you that I'm completely healed, it sells more
books, but healing is a journey that never ends, it's called LIFE.
Know your condition. Know you are now a survivor and wear
your scars bravely. Some scars will heal, others will take time.

You will have peaks and troughs but you will know that you are not the same person you were. You have grown and the bad times become less. All you have to do is to trust the process that you are undergoing and know that you are becoming more than you ever imagined you could be.

I am in a house now that supports my healing, I have given myself a year without work, without a career and without income and ageing fast. It is a terrifying place this going dry on my busyness. Yet it is the only place I can be so that I can feel the damage in my body, mind and soul and address it. My mind, within a matter of months, has become calmer and depression has mainly gone. There are days when I can't stand the boredom and I know on those days that my fears are near the surface. As the months go by I am confronted by many things mainly I understand why people keep busy, why the world is so fast. Everyone is running away from the real truth that life is, in fact, very hard and sometimes unendurable. When there is little to do you are confronted with yourself and if you don't like yourself its not great company.

Here in this house with its healing garden I grow herbs and watch the birds fly in the blue sky. I sit in the sun and meditate and dig the earth with my hands. All the things that I had run away from in order not to be like my family, mundane, have come back for me to get to know and to embrace. I now have time to write which is something I have always loved and should have done a long time ago.

I take a break from my writing to walk to the shop and get some treats for the evening, strawberries and pannacotta. There is a song playing in the shop by Robert Palmer called 'Every kind of people', and it reminds me of other days from my past and makes me think of the meaning of the words.

Returning home the sun comes out and I feel its warmth. I realise as I walk back how very lucky I am to now be free from friends, family and places that imprisoned me and it makes me smile and puts a spring in my step. I am free from the naivety of my youth and now being awake to life and how it really is has sharpened and defined what choices I make and makes me realise that I have had the chance to start again.

I have been given a chance to start again without her. The opportunity to thrive is slowly becoming within my grasp. I will start and stop and falter but if I read my journal I see how far I have actually come. Making a new and better life for that child who was suffering and giving her all that she rightly deserves.

In writing this book I have re-lived some sad moments but it has given me a new vision of where I am right now. I look back at my past and to when it all began to unravel for me and see that I am not the same person. I thought I had been standing still and instead see that I have grown and healed much more than I realised.

When you walk this path your strength returns and when it does you can write your story and pass it on. You can do all the things that you dared not do and most of all you can understand who you truly are and what your purpose in life is, beyond the bars of the prison you have freed yourself from.

Seeking help

When you begin on your journey of healing you may look for a therapist or help online. Use as much discriminating awareness as you would when meeting any new person. This is because there are many therapists who also have this disorder of NPD and I have met some, both off and online.

I met a lady online who claimed to be an expert on the subject because of her own experience with men with NPD. After speaking to her for some time, or rather it was her who spoke all the time, I noticed how she was behaving. She would not turn up for a Skype appointment again and again leaving me abandoned not knowing why. Then she would say she had forgotten or try to make out it was my fault. Then after a while I noticed that she got a bit angry when the conversation wasn't going fast enough or I wasn't saying what she wanted to hear. Most of the time she spent talking at me and although what she said made sense I didn't really want advice, I wanted support or a caring ear. So I ended it, but not after having been shafted by a narcissist at a time when I was at my lowest ebb.

There are many men and also women who are writing books on the subject of NPD who actually have the disorder themselves, imagine that!. There are also several YouTube channels which are run by narcissist men or women so use your time wisely by checking out these people. Reading or hearing the words of someone who has a personality disorder will take you right into their mind. They have interesting things to say on the subject. However on a subtle level I find that very disturbing.

When you go to a therapist ask them a lot of questions about themselves and if they act uncomfortable about that head on out very quickly. Take note of how they look, where they live and how open they are. It is also as well to know that a good therapist is able to verbalise their own boundaries.

If by chance you do make the mistake, (we all do it), of finding a narcissistic therapist it can also help you to recognise that you are still open to narcissists and will give you an indicator as to how you are progressing.

PART 2

Healing a lifetime of depression and abuse

Survivors

To all the brave survivors of sexual, emotional, violent, ritual, mind control, narcissistic abuse. The ones who made it and the ones who didn't. For the courageous people who stand up and fight on behalf of those who are unable to do so. The silenced ones, the sick ones, those locked in mental institutions, care homes and prisons of all kinds. To the survivors who roam the streets without a home. For those with a home but unable to escape the abuse within. For all survivors everywhere who find themselves in this realm of suffering. You will heal over time though it may not seem it right now. Your scars will be a sign of your courage when you realise what you have endured. Only time will tell why you have woken up and what your path will finally be.

YOU ARE NOT ALONE

Dimly lit Passage

It is dark in here,
dark and lonely.
I long for the light,
I long for the light of her smile,
to take me out
of this living hell.
But she never came,
she never came to rescue me,
so I must stay and wait,
and want.
Here
in this dark, dank place
they call hell,
the basement of all minds.
Further into the earth,
further and further
away from the light
and into the darkness of her smile
as she turns away
from the child she hates.

Alice Little

Depression

'It's black isn't it and grey sometimes or even red but somehow white or yellow are never on the depression palette'.
Alice Little

Depression that awful black word that speaks volumes. Yet it remains silent and secret, in it's host, a whispered secret of an illness too gloomy to speak about, too self absorbed in it's nature to admit. If this were an illness of body it would be rewarded with sympathy and understanding. But this disease is not a cancer or physical illness anyone can see, yet it acts as if it were, a cancer of the mind, body and spirit, because it infects all three and disables and takes away the ability to live fully.

As with any mental illness it comes in many forms that run on a spectrum from mild to untreatable. It is always embarrassing for those who have it and also for those who meet with them and do not understand. Illness of a mental nature is slowly being understood and accepted but still has attached to it the stigma of madness and the days of Bedlam and fear.

I hid my illness, sometimes I hid it from myself because I wanted to be normal, I wanted to partake of a life that others seem to be living, even when I knew that that was not entirely true. Seemingly happy lives on the outside can often hide underlying suffering. Those around you can also suffer because of your depression and unless you have the support of loving partners or friends it can be a very lonely road.

Depression has been my constant companion for all my teenage and adult life. It has dulled the edges of my experience and brought with it devastating life changes because of making decisions when in the wrong frame of mind, meeting the wrong kind of people while not aware and creating a barrier between myself and the world.

Having explored the origins of my depression, which deal with narcissistic, sexual, emotional and ritual abuse, I have come to a point of healing in which I am now able to write down my experiences of how I became depressed and my road to healing.

I am no longer depressed and suicidal every day, in fact, my life is quite uneventful. As I recovered from depression I found that my life was no longer filled with drama, the drama that depression creates. Depression is addictive and acts like a host within its victim eating away at the mind, pretending to be a helpful ally that gives some meaning to an otherwise boring existence.

It is hard to let go of depression so you have to starve it of its supply because depression is the narcissist within and it is therefore not you. No amount of positive thinking helped me, nor therapy, it was a natural progression. I took away the negative narcissistic people in my life, took away my coping device (workaholic-ism) and starved depression of its fix.

My depression started very early on in my life but I was not aware that it had a name, that awful sadness. As a child any sign of emotion good or bad was stamped upon and denied. My parents, both of whom denied their feelings, also denied mine as did all members of my family. The coldness and indifference that they showed me during times of stress compounded the effect that my feelings were not right or untrue.

My grandmother who did show great love to me was, none the less, a victim of her time. Trans-generational dynamics were passed on and codes of conduct had to be adhered to. Even she, who loved me when no one else did, in the end could not help me and I was made to uphold the family tradition of pretending that my family was a good family, a family that was upstanding within the community. Shaming or denying of this pretend family resulted in shunning me and I became the black sheep of the family. I wore for them all the disowned, disgraced and hidden evils that they were hiding. I was cast out and I cast myself out eventually.

I was the lucky one, I was able to escape while every other member of my family, the cult of cults, remained brainwashed and asleep, while I was to wake up. So I guess I should be thankful to them for sending me out into the dessert with their blackness and sin pinned onto me, they did me a favour. So I have the last laugh! I felt sorry for those Pavlovian Dogs I left behind. I even imagined saving them from the family cult but now I know that I can't.

I am coping with life without depression, a new way of living. I stay aware that it lies deep within my psyche and am watchful of it trying to appear. It is a bit like trying to cut ivy or weeds from a garden, they appear in another place.

This is my story and each person's story is unique, yours will be too. You may find some similarities in my story but you may also find points which you don't comprehend or understand, none the less it is my truth as it happened to me. Please take from it that which inspires you on your journey and leave that which you do not resonate with, perhaps to be read at some time in the future.

So let me take you into my world.!

Perfumed

I smell her smell,
it is unique,
like a sweet?
No,
perhaps flowers?
It is a bottle
of mother.
Only she has it,
it is a one off.
Just thinking about it,
makes her come to mind.
Her stench,
of untrustworthy
violence.

Alice Little

The cruelty of my mother

'Some people try to be tall by cutting off the heads of others'
Tibetan Buddhist saying

The white cotton handkerchief that she puts in my mouth, bound and tied at the back of my head, stops me from making a noise, the object and reason of her torture. I like to sing and dance but she hates it, hates to see my free spirit, wants to chain it and stamp it out. When she is finished her tying I can't swallow because the handkerchief absorbs the moisture in my mouth. I am terrified as she stands in front of me berating me, teaching me a lesson, her eyes wide and staring and finger pointing as she spits her venom on me. Then on cue my anxiety levels taken to new heights, my eyes roll back and I am taken into the bliss of unconsciousness. Her job is now done.

I find it hard to let go of the good mother image I have in my mind, the good mother who would never do such a cruel thing. No, this is not my mother it is a demon. So it begins, the splitting of good and bad parents that I will continue to live with right into adulthood.

There was a lot of cruelty in the things that my parents did to me. I believe that I reminded them of a free self they no longer or, if ever, had. At a time when children should be 'seen and not heard', I too was also taught not to be seen. So I learned to become invisible not noticed and it became a learned part of my personality.

I understand that my parents must have had terrible childhoods themselves and I have compassion for them but they inflicted their stuff onto me and they have no regret for doing so nor would they admit to it. I ask you,would I be in such a mess if it were not true?

The above story is one of many little sinister events that shaped my mind as it is today. I have spent most of my adult life trying to overcome that legacy of suppression and just when I get there, I stop myself. I get to a barrier where the demons and dragons that seem to guard the place I try to get to will not let me pass, so I turn around and go back, another 'Ground-hog Day'. Only this time I have become stronger, it's just that I can forget how far I have actually come. I am, in fact, not standing still but have moved miles without realising.

A mother's cruelty?

Contemplation

I'm going to pose a few questions to you to ask yourself. In asking yourself these questions you will be looking at the relationship with your mother to find out if it is toxic.

Could you change the way you think about yourself?
How could you change your way of thinking?
Do you feel that your thinking is outside yourself?
How would your mother respond if you changed?

Do you ever ask yourself any of these questions or pose statements similar to this?

Did my mother abuse me?
Was I a bad child and deserving of being hit?
Why couldn't I have been kinder to my mother?
If only I had tried harder
I know my mother loves me, only she had a hard life
My mother never hit me
I am a bad person and don't deserve love
The next time we speak I am going to try harder
If only I were taller, smaller, brighter, prettier,less attractive.
I'm ugly
My mother doesn't mean to say unkind things to me
I feel sorry for my mother.
I'm going to make her proud of me
I'm going to stop telling her about my achievements
I'm going to dress down a bit
My mother hates me
My mother dissaproves of me
I hate my mother
I want to leave home
I never want to see my mother again

Look at your self-talk and investigate whether it is true or false. Go through each statement and tick which ones resonate with you and see if you can find a pattern of thinking. When you find that pattern see if you can relate it to any events from your childhood and how this thinking has affected your life. Add a few of your own 'stinking thinking' thought patterns to this list. Keep going, don't stop. When you can't write any more take your list read through it and then re-write every sentence with a positive quote. Then take one of the positive statements and write it down and read it for a week. Keep the negative statement to one side but don't read it again. After a week look at the negative statement and see if it has decreased in power. Put the positive statement next to it and see which is the strongest. You can repeat this with all of the negative quotes you make about yourself.

Here is an example:

Was I a bad child and deserved to be hit?

Let's explore this. As a child you are in a development stage. Your hearing,speaking and understanding of life and what adults do is a mystery. You see the world in a different way to them. When they want you to do something it should be with an understanding that you are not an adult. You need to be spoken to with patience in the knowledge that you may not understand and may need to be told many times before you do. You may also need to be spoken to in a way that is easy to understand for you and not from an adult's perspective.

If this doesn't happen and instead you are shouted at or beaten you will become stressed and it will be even harder for you to understand. If you were being abused by an adult you would already be very stressed and your development may have been thwarted by the abuse, making it hard for you to concentrate.

You may even have developed an angry or aggressive side to cope with your abuse. If the adults who are bringing you up didn't see this or were your abusers and didn't care then you, as a child, were not to blame for any coping devices that you created to survive. You are also not to blame for any reaction to their behaviour towards you.

Conclusion:

You were not a bad child deserving to be hit
You were a child who deserved care and understanding.
You were a good child who tried their best
You were too young to understand
You were not to blame for the adult's anger
You were not to blame for their abuse of you

Empty

I could die of
this sadness,
that crushes my soul.
I could drown,
in my tears,
for lack of love.
There is no one here
but me.
No one cares.
Oh! save me
from this empty planet,
that is me,
that is inside me.

Alice Little

The bear who abused me

"You love it don't you? You love to make me hit you".
'Mommie Dearest' film dialogue

The large brown teddy that is my favourite toy is also a toy I am deeply afraid of. My mother uses it as a form of control because it is watching me all the time and will tell her what I have been up to. I both love and hate this toy. It goes with me everywhere, she makes sure of that, watching and spying on me. Sometimes it appears as the nice teddy it really is and I now see that I projected onto it the split personality of my mother, appearing to be benevolent and kind then changing in a moment to cruel and violent.

To use a child's cuddly toy to manipulate and control them seems to be the most sinister of things to do to a child. If you have a toy which you have had since a child perhaps you could ask yourself, or it, what it knows. Does its cuddly exterior hold a more sinister side, one which you have hidden from yourself?

Telling a child that their toys come alive when they are asleep has got to be the stupidest form of control and brain washing ever. It is not a cute fairy tale, it's a lie. The amount of lies parents tell their children is awful and if you can make a child believe in lies and get them to use their imaginations to create false truths imagine what else you can scare them with and get them to believe in.

When I looked at the reality of what my mother had been doing in using this toy as a cruel form of child abuse I cut off its head. I know that sounds shocking but once I admitted to myself what it had been used for and all the memories it held for me I couldn't have it in my life. So I cut it up along with all the photos of my childhood and my past and put them in a great heap to be disposed of. I did wonder afterwards about all the pictures I had destroyed but I found they were in my memory anyway. I don't regret the destruction of my toy or the photographs.

Strangely enough I found a new toy who I loved very much who also talked to me and it wasn't until he hit me one day (don't worry I know it was me really!) that I realised that this wasn't right, it was too weird and I started to explore how my mother had used my teddy to control me. The toy I have now is in a box. I haven't destroyed him because he holds a key to my past via the present and when I can bear to look at that I will.

I wonder how many other childhood toys there are around that hold memories to our past. Have you got one?

Bad House move

This house is not my home
I hate it,
yet it holds me,
makes me stay another day.
It is filled with the rotten stench
of the past,
of the trials,
of previous owners,
who all struggled
to leave it.
A coffin arrives
they leave.
They should have left sooner,
getting rid of their horrible old
festering tat,
instead of leaving it to
their children.
Instead of leaving their decay
for me to transform.
Born into and raised in such
evil, dark, ugly places
I roam looking
for home.
But I only find
the misery of others
which I have to clean
and scrub and
resurrect.

Alice Little

Letting go of your 'emotional materialism'©

'Clutter is always about loss, what or whom did you loose, that's your answer'.
Alice Little

If you decide to get rid of old photos, toys, or anything else connected to your childhood, throwing them away will not necessarily get rid of the memory or the emotion. This takes time. The right time to let go of things may be when the image or item no longer holds a huge emotional charge for you. Getting rid of old clutter will help you move on and allow room for the vacuum you create. By doing this you allow something new to enter your life.

'Emotional Materialism'© is a name I gave to the items we keep and hoard which have an emotional charge and link to memories from the past. These are items which may not be of any use to us but we are unable, however, to let go of them. It also refers to collections of items which the collector is unable to stop collecting or letting go of.

Letting go of old stuff connected to your past can be difficult but it is very liberating. On a spectrum scale, collecting and hoarding are a sign of mental disorders, starting with a few things, then gradually increasing, they are always connected with loss.

Consider for a moment all the things that you have in your home and ask yourself this question,

Do I love, like or need them?
If you don't like them ask yourself why do you have them in your home?

I had a special family heirloom in my house. I neither liked it nor wanted it but because it had been given to me, I kept it. It was on display for a while and then ended up stored in my loft and carted round from house to house as I moved. When I started to

105

focus on my abusive family I really looked at the item and decided to get rid of it. At one time it was worth some money but by the time I sold it it was worthless being out of fashion and, dare I say it, - ugly! Do I regret it, NO! I haven't missed it nor do I want to be reminded of an unhappy childhood every time I would have seen it.

If you are very attached to your stuff and know you should let it go but can't, here is a simple way to start.

Getting a friend to help who is supportive or a counsellor is a good idea, but if you don't have a friend who can help you don't let that stop you from beginning.

How to let go

If you don't know where to start, start small, with just a few papers you can tidy and sort out or perhaps a desk top or a shelf that needs attention.

When you are ready to do more here is a good way to begin.

Take three boxes.
Put a label on each box

- one says **don't know**
- one says **no**
- one says **throw**

Keep the boxes well away from each other and mark them with large letters. Having each one a different colour helps but if that isn't possible you could add a colour in another way to help you distinguish each box.

The **don't know** box is for items that you **don't know** if you want to throw out or not. You can look in this box again later.

The **no** box is for items that you **do not want** to get rid of.

The **throw** box is for items that you **want** to get rid of.

You will need to do this process several times and regularly.

It can be very exhausting to do this exercise so make sure you allow some time to rest, write and recuperate afterwards.

If you can't even do the exercise above you can also call your local council who have a team dedicated to this service. You can also hire someone who advertises themselves as a 'Clutter Clearer'

When you start to clear out your clutter the effect is that it allows space for new things to enter your life. You stop living in your past and move into a better future. If you keep your clutter you create a heavy, depressed, atmosphere in your home and mind. So here is a reminder about what clutter is.

IF YOU DON'T LIKE IT OR YOU DON'T LOVE IT THROW IT OR GIVE IT AWAY!!!!

Twitch

I saw her twitch
out of the corner
of my eye.
On the bus,
saw her,
knew why.
Takes away the pain,
creates a distraction
for the mind's
suffering.
Like self-harming.
Displacements we do,
she did.
She's enjoying it
I thought.
Feeling glad that I
no longer allow
myself to twitch
as a habit.
Perhaps she has Parkinson's?
Whatever it is
I believe it is holding pain.
We all hide our pain,
by displacing,
loosing self,
spinning out.
Get lost!

Alice Little

My Mother, sexual abuse

'Focus on the reasons you should leave and not on the reasons you should stay'.
Alice Little

I felt my mother's hatred of me in every look she gave me, in every word she uttered my way and in every act of violence she did to me. But mostly I felt her hatred of me in the fact that she regularly sexually abused me and I knew then that I was a disgusting, dirty, despicable creature undeserved of love. I would be physically sick after she had put her hands on me and for that I would be beaten. Abused, disgraced and beaten I would retreat into my own world spending time alone with no one to turn to or talk to, a forbidden subject. I did tell once about her abuse and also the abuse of other members of my family but my grandmother, who I told, took me to the priest who made me wash out my mouth and said he would have to exorcise the demons within me and that I was a wicked child who told lies. This was the same priest who also sexually abused me.

My mother did many awful things to me but perhaps the worst betrayal was that she sexually abused me. Sexual abuse by your mother really messes up your mind because you can't believe it, all you can do is go along with it because, even though you don't feel it is right, you have no choice and it is what you come to understand to be affection and attention.

I found it hard to go to sleep as a child because I was too stressed and too over stimulated by the beatings and abuse. So to get me to sleep my mother would penetrate me digitally, if I didn't show signs of sleep she would do it more and more aggressively until I did. Eventually I would split, not sleep, but split and I am sure that this happened most nights though I only remember a few occasions. It is a most shaming and uncomfortable thing to remember and recount here, even after so long. Just to think of it makes my flesh crawl.

109

As I got older she would use my body to get sexual pleasure for herself by rubbing me up against her. It would start off as a game and I would play along because I was getting some affection from her. When she had finished with me she cast me aside with a sweep of her arm and told me I was disgusting. I felt it was somehow my fault and didn't know what I had done wrong.

I was very unhealthily enmeshed with my mother. I had no idea where I started and she left off. I only knew her world, the make believe one she had taught me, and so I lived my life through her and for her, never experiencing life through my own eyes. So when she up and left I was devastated and never got over losing her.

When I got older and stopped pretending that she was perfect and some sort of angel, things changed because I was changing. My mother didn't like me changing. She preferred that I carry on pretending that I was the person she had made me into. I was more than that as I had been independent for so long, having to look after myself, that despite her early mind control I was my own person. It's just that my independence had not fully developed.

When I confronted her about her abuse she cut me out of her life for over 10 years until I made the mistake of contacting her. Yet it wasn't really a mistake because during that time I found out who she really was. I had had a long time away from her and this time I was awake and could see through her. I had no idea that what I was experiencing was narcissistic abuse but as soon as I found out it was as if a light went on and finally I was able to let go of her and my family for good.

110

Waiting

Waiting for death,
waiting for life,
stuck in the middle.
No small opening
to climb through
and escape.
The every day prison
that holds me
brings locks to hold my body
till it hurts.
Puts metal helmets
on my head
till it hurts.
Sends noises and shouts
and uncomfortable sounds
so that
I can no longer hear.
Sends images to my eyes
that, worn with age,
can no longer
and no longer
want to see.
I wait for you.

Alice Little

The cruelty of my father

'There is a twisted enjoyment to my fathers games that I do not share'
Alice Little

It is a hot, dry summer day and the dust from the room is in the air, I cough. I am four years old. My father tells me to lie on edge of the rug and I cry knowing what will come next. I have to lie still and stillness is something I find hard, because I love to move. He wants to stop me moving and he wants to torture me, this man who looks so nice on the outside, just like my mother, he is not my father either, he is also a demon. He makes me put my arms by my side and as I do he rolls me up in the rug, over and over I go until I am bound up in it and unable to move at all. He enjoys my terror, it makes him laugh and I am confused by his laughter because it is not funny to me. I have to beg him to let me out and that pleases him. The next time he does it he makes sure my head is below the edge of the carpet and I feel as if I am suffocating, the dust makes me cough. It is dark in here and I am scared. I don't know where I am and become disorientated as he rolls the rug over. Then he stops and leaves me there, it is no fun if I am not crying. But I have disappeared now, I am not there any more, I remember nothing after this because I have split off, dissociated.

When I became older I learned about disassociation and splitting because I became aware that I was still doing it and although it helped me then, it was not helping now. I was splitting off and not paying attention just like I did at school, not able to listen or take in what was being said to me. I was often beaten at school with a ruler or a strap by the teachers, because that was the punishment then. My hands had become clenched and it took many sessions with a body worker to get me to let go and relax them. Now as I type I have hot pains in my fingers and my arms and neck hurt as the legacy they left returns again and again. I have to remember to relax and only then does the pain of holding disappear.

As time goes on, whenever I get anxious, I learn to hold my breath and my body. Deep hidden scars lie within my cells waiting to be detonated by the right circumstances. The rug rolling torture was done many times and each time I would pass out sooner and sooner until just the mere idea of it would make me faint.

Parents hide their cruelty in seemingly playful games and jokes that they find funny, but are not so funny to a small child. I avoid watching programmes on TV that include pranks made on small children because I know the price that will be paid when they become an adult.

My father's Narcissistic Abuse took a different form to that of my mother because he would manipulate instead of using violence and torture me in the guise of playing a game, he could even do it in front of others.

I always lost it with my father and I thought that was because I was a feisty individual but now I know that he was manipulating me and enjoying my anger and frustration. My anger was fuel for him, the narcissistic supply. He would let me rant on for ages and all the while he would remain deadly silent, until I stopped and realised that I was in a monologue.

I got nowhere with any dialogue or argument. All I got was to feel bad about myself and found I was right back where I had started. He had this ability to manipulate me even as I got older but the last time he did so the penny dropped and I never ever contacted him again nor any of his flying monkeys, my family.

What a win for me!

Suicide

There are days when
I think of suicide,
I admit it.
I know,
I feel shame.
But I would not be alone,
would I?
When I go into my mind,
looking for doors,
to escape the suffering I feel,
I sometimes end up
in the middle of a maze.
A maze where all exits,
are blocked.
I am locked in the claustrophobia
of my own mind.
No escape,only death
Ah! what a relief.
There is a door,
but it is a door to avoid.
I touch it,
stare at it,
I know it well.
But I will never
walk through it.
The door marked,
'SUICIDE'

Alice Little

Gaslighting

'Practical jokes and put downs may make others laugh but the recipient hides the hurt they really feel'
Alice Little

When my father gets his camera out it means trouble. He looks around to see if anyone is watching even in this desolate forsaken place that we live in. I am four years old and have on my best dress and want to run around and play but playing always irritates my parents, in fact, everything irritates my parents but mostly I do. He grabs my hand and coaxes me towards the car. I hate his car because he uses it for so many things, taking me to horrid relatives, abusive men and also as a vehicle in which to abuse me hidden and out of sight, his very own torture chamber. He often locks me in and loves to see me cry and shout. When he releases me he becomes my saviour because I have nowhere to turn to. I don't understand at this age that it is abuse, I just don't understand, so I internalise it as a form of madness. But today he has a special treat in store for me because he puts me in the boot with a premise of taking a picture. I have no choice because if I don't he will close the lid and leave me there just like he has just shown me, a warning of what will happen if I don't comply. Soon he will not need to threaten because I will become more compliant with just a look. He can then take pictures of me in any pose he wants and with whoever he wants. Doing whatever he asks. Somewhere there are pictures of me that I would not like to see.

My father only had to look at me and I was controlled by that look. His narcissistic abuse was quite different from my mother's in that he not only hid it from the outside but he also hid it from me. I didn't know that what I was receiving was abuse because he would wrap it up in something else so that I didn't know that what he was doing was Gaslighting. In Gaslighting the narcissist over-writes your reality with theirs. When Gaslighting occurs it

115

happens in stages, the first one being a knowledge of something 'off' happening, something that didn't feel right or odd and yet you discount it or don't believe it happened. The next stage is when you defend their action by confronting them and being defensive, while the narcissist will deny or minimise everything you say.

This form of denial starts to nag at your mind as you go over and over again the conversation or the event. You know that what is happening or has happened is not right but you are at the stage where you still believe that it is your fault. You then start to behave strangely and your world feels crazy. It is difficult to talk to anyone about it because, not only do you feel its partly your fault, but you are afraid to or, if you do, they may not understand and can also think there is something wrong with you.

You will try to appease and please the narcissist to gain their approval. You will change your behaviour and the way you dress but, most sadly, you will change your mind and your reality to theirs. Then you fall into an apathy of depression and self-hatred when your former self is disappearing and you start to become the person they say you are, worthless.

The suppression that abuse creates lasts a lifetime. It seems sometimes as if there is no time off from it. The narcissist parent creates suppression buttons which are installed to be set off at a required time, when they want you to do something you don't want to do. You have been brainwashed and don't know it because you are too young and too impressionable.

My father denied everything. Nothing he ever said was the truth and if something needed to be said he would get someone else to say it for him or he would tell you without looking at you. I never felt comfortable communicating with my father because it would always end in an argument. His way of controlling me.

My father was rarely affectionate and was always absent so I had a deep longing in me for his love which I never received. He never ever gave me credit for anything I did, only put downs. He laughed at everything I did and gave me no praise, support or advice other than criticism.

I used to cry just looking at him from afar because it was a loss to me, my emotionally unavailable absent father. It was not until I began looking at that later in my life that I realised it just didn't make sense. I didn't know why I cried for him even when he was present in the flesh but now I know.

My father, sexual abuse

'Parents who sexually abuse their children, you call it what you want, it's still rape'.
Alice Little

It is always the same, same time, same routine. He has been working nights and must stop off for a drink on the way home. He's not an alcoholic but still he smells of drink. I will have been lying awake waiting to hear his key in the door. He comes upstairs to hang up his coat but before he does that he comes in to see me. I can smell smoke and perfume on his coat and drink on his breath. He kneels down and kisses me with his horrid breath and scratchy moustache and his hands frantically search for my vagina. He rubs me hard and whispers my name. "Come on" he says quickly and he waits until my orgasm has reached. Within a moment he has left me staring at the ceiling, unable to describe my feelings or my shame at what I feel I have done.

Sexual abuse is dirty, it leaves you feeling dirty. While they touch you and mostly when they stop and walk away because it is then that they lay their shame on you. They believe that it is your fault and so do you.

My father's sexual abuse was not limited to this incidence. It went on from very early childhood and only stopped when I started my periods at 11 years old. I also think that at this time he replaced me in his dirty sexual affections with my brother.

As an adult I confronted him about it but he just laughed in my face and said prove it. Historic abuse is abuse that they think they have got away with and they usually have. They rely on your silence and your forgetting the incident in order to cope with life.

Coping is not a life, it is a way of making you ill in body mind and spirit. It robs you of a full life and then robs you when you get older because it is only then that you can bear the burden of looking at it and healing from it.

I don't feel the need to write down a description of every single story of my sexual abuse because I have spent so long in therapy and so long healing it that I have left it now to history. The beginning of my healing of this abuse happened when I first told my husband that a family member had abused me and I had never told anyone before, ever.

Then I started to get flashbacks, which lasted years, of events that I had half remembered and half forgotten. Memories which I had tried to avoid looking at now came up for me to purify. Those years were very intense and the emotions and pain that I lived through were, at times, unbearable. Not only had I been abused once but now I was having to re-live it all over again.

The sexual abuse was something that I healed and moved on from as much as I could, as much as you can from this stuff. Now I am trying to heal from the narcissistic abuse that was also part of this sickness my parents and family had and have. This is called Narcissistic Personality Disorder and it is only something that I discovered as I got older and I suppose am able to cope with. It is the most evil of possessions because it enters a child's whole being and destroys who they are or could become.

This kind of abuse goes hand in hand with any other abuse because in order to be cruel you would have to have no empathy and abusers have none. It was not until I went No Contact with my family, leaving everything I had known behind that I started to really heal.

I have found that healing comes in waves. You heal from one part or at least it has less effect on your life. Then another part of your life comes up to be looked at. For me I know it is only part of growing and waking up. There is no actual end. Certainly there is a growth.

Narcissistic Abuse

'When you were born you became, not your mother's beloved daughter, but the enemy, the competition'.
Alice Little

I am playing with my toys sat on the floor and my mother bends over me. I look up and smile and she slaps me hard on the face. I don't know what I have done wrong and I cry and now she is really angry. Then she smiles and I'm really scared.

I am lying in bed and she is stroking my face gently and then slaps it hard and she does it again and again and again, until I am so scared of any touch from her or anyone else.

Both my parents and many of my family had Narcissistic Personality Disorder. I don't mean just a healthy amount of narcissism like we all have, I mean a real personality disorder. My family hid behind a persona of normality in public but behind closed doors it was different, which makes it really hard to get anyone to believe you.

The parents who could actually say they loved me in reality hated me. It is a hard fact to even admit this to yourself and this is how they keep you hooked in to them, making it hard to leave. But I did leave them for good once I woke up and realised that I no longer wanted to be abused by them.

I didn't realise when I left them that what they had was NPD. It wasn't until later on that I realised that something about them was really 'off' and I started to explore what that was. I was shocked to find that NPD was exactly what they had and, all of a sudden, it all made sense. **I wasn't crazy, they were!**

The sexual abuse was clear cut, I (sort of) understood it, but the emotional abuse didn't make any sense at all. They had placed their crazy on me and I hadn't realised, it was only then that I started to heal.

Zombie

It beckons its long fingers
tries to lead me,
take me with it.
Die like it,
like them,
zombies,
stealing my life.
Death robs,
I want life,
but suicide tempts.
It is an ache in my heart,
a longing to fulfil
the legacy.
They want me to
kill myself,
hand me a knife to do it.
But I am weak
and afraid to die.
So I stay alive,
a Zombie,
like them.

Alice Little

Ritual abuse and mind control

'Control of your mind is their ultimate goal and it should be your goal too'.
Alice Little

The cloth that I lie on does not take away the coldness of the concrete slab underneath my body. This cold deathly grey slab that I will die upon. There are people in the room, murmurs of words I can not hear or understand. They are singing or chanting or shouting but I can't hear, I am deaf with fear. The man who stands above me has eyes that look as if they are non human or from a horror film, surely no one can look this evil. His lips pull back and I see his gruesome grin of teeth, bad teeth. As he utters words above me, the sound still muffled though I can tell it is getting louder. I try to close my eyes but I can't, they won't let me. I have to see what he is about to do. His hand rises up and I see in his hand a large knife which is held above my heart. The knife comes down and I am dead.

I tell this story to my counsellor and she makes me go back and see it again. This time I am safe because she is supportive. As I recount the story and see it in my mind she asks me to tell her where the knife goes and I don't know. Look again she says and this time I realise that the knife goes down by the side of the altar. She has helped me to see this without actually telling me and I am amazed. As I am still alive it all makes sense that this was a ritual not to kill me, but to split me.

This haunting picture has scared me for years and now I feel the emotional charge that it had, slip away. Once I had researched why they would have done this to me, I understand that it is to create alters within me, ready to invoke when the time comes. A sub-personality that can act outside of myself, beyond myself. They split my mind into many, many parts using mind control and abuse.

The grey concrete slab is in the basement of my aunt's house, we children play there even though we shouldn't. In the cupboards are gold chalices and other strange items I do not recognise. I do not associate this room with the ritual that I underwent until much later in my life when I wonder how I could have forgotten.

Ritual abuse is something that is denied. Child abuse used to be denied but now is coming out. Eventually ritual abuse will be outed too. Cruelty to animals, bestiality, yes another taboo subject. I hope in the future that shameful subjects will be more addressed. Wouldn't it be great if society decided to become good, together!

Other Me

They made me go away
they put me somewhere hidden.
So deep inside
that I lost myself.
I didn't know I was lost,
yet part of me,
was always looking,
trying to find something.
A seeker.
I just didn't know,
that what I was
looking for,
was myself.

Alice Little

Dying to myself

'They made me go away, disappear, but I found out where they had hidden me'.
Alice Little

I am lying in a long box made of wood, the room is old and dark, it seems like night. I have got so used to dissociating that I am pliable to do anything and not question. I have also been given alcohol and a drug in a clear liquid form. My hands are on my chest holding a small candle which is lit. I do not remember the people only the act. They close the box lid, it is a coffin, telling me that when the candle goes out I will be reborn. Then the candle does go out, I am shut in the box and I black out, I remember nothing after apart from someone calling me a name I did not recognise.

Ritual abuse is totally discounted as an event that happened and is happening. No one believes that something so awful could exist. Those who choose to hide it do so by bringing forward stories of ritual abuse that will have no credence. This is disinformation and it is what keeps it hidden and surviving.

It is nothing other than mind control abuse. It has many levels. Those on the lower level are just playing at it but those at the top are not playing. They use it for murder, blackmail, sex, prostitution and mainly money and the degradation of those who are abused. Creating a sub-culture of humans without empathy and willing to do anything they are bid.

Something was protecting me then because, even though my mental health has suffered, I have not degraded myself nor turned to their ways.

When I first started to remember the ritual abuse I was not in therapy and I could not find a therapist to help me. I had half memories of my childhood that didn't make sense. Like the stories above. Now those memories were being opened out and revealed to me. Eventually I found a lady in central London, the only person in the UK. Just before I was due to travel to London I got a call from her letting me know that she was having to disappear as there was a smear campaign against her and it would be in the papers. She told me that there would be many articles in the paper discrediting survivor's accounts of their abuse particularly Ritual Abuse and to be brave.

She was right. Many articles came out and the effect on me and other survivors was enormous. No one ever believes, not even today. So I had to be my own therapist and dealing with this sort of stuff was terrifying. Eventually I found a therapist but mainly any ritual abuse I disclosed was sort of discounted a bit as adult games. Perhaps she had no experience of it or perhaps she was one of the therapists you hear about who do know about it and are part of it, keeping a lid on it and keeping you quiet. It's hard to tell.

It happens gradually

It is dark in this hole and I am afraid but the other older children who are talking to me are telling me about fairies and fairies are always linked with mushrooms. They pass me down a mushroom to eat and I am too young to know that these are no ordinary mushrooms but are what they refer to as magic mushrooms. I can see a light at the top of the hole where the children are standing and then an older voice and the children all start to tell a story together. When the story is finished they throw earth on top of me and close the light off by shutting the entrance. I am terrified and scream and shout. I have been buried alive. Then in an instant hundreds of fairies appear and I pass out and remember nothing.

Fairies

If you are reading this now and you love fairies or are following a 'Faery' tradition, which is fashionable at present, you may not like to hear my experience of fairies. No one likes to have their world shattered, or their belief in what they believe in shattered, but this is my story and what actually happened to me. It is up to you what you believe in.

Ritual Abuse is never done immediately just like the grooming of child sexual abuse victims (part of ritual abuse). It is done in stages to make the victim more pliable and suggestive to actions and ideas. Before taking the child into the terror of Ritual Abuse they may be primed first by the luring of fairies, that's how it happened to me.

It is despicable that pretty things like fairies are used to lure children into a much darker practice, that of Satanic Ritual Abuse. This is how I was brainwashed. My mother being the main culprit of stupid fairy lies where she created scenarios to make me believe in their existence. To this day I can't go near anything fairy.

I was led into the realm of fairies first to prime me and anaesthetise me to the further realms which would get progressively darker.

All of the experiences I had during Ritual Abuse were of a dark, deviant, sexual and evil nature. I was being groomed for use both as a child but also for later on in my life when I would be used by men for sex. The victim is abused so that they will have so little self respect that they will do anything to achieve the desire of the abuser no matter what age they become. Many end up in prostitution.

The next stage was the use of angels and this I find too difficult to even write about. The last stage is an introduction to the devil himself and just to speak that name or think about it makes me immediately remember that I am a being of light and goodness and I am protected.

My hope is that these stories I am telling in this book will be understood as part of a greater sickness within our society. I have only revealed a few and I also do not, nor want to, have a full recollection of this most damaging types of abuse. If you would like to research this subject further there are now many sites on the internet with reference to Ritual Abuse. Not all are authentic and you should be discriminating in your choice.

Mind Control

'The sun shining through the gap in the clouds was my focus even in the darkest nights of my suffering'.
Alice Little

There is a tall grey box in my aunt's house. It has a glass window in it and a small shelf at the front. It looks a bit like a ticket box where you might pay at at the cinema. But this box is for me. I sit inside the box which has a tall seat in and look out of the window. I can not see who it is outside because it is a blank in my mind. The person outside is holding up different cards for me to look at with symbols on. I can not hear anything and I become afraid. Someone comes into the box and talks to me, I don't remember what they say but I know they are mad. I have to look at blank, white cards and hold up the cards they have given me with symbols on telling them what I think is on the other side. It is totally exhausting and I blank out after this remembering nothing before or after. It is an image that confused me and I ignored it for years.

Although my self esteem was not great, obviously they couldn't get to me like they did others. There was something they wanted that I wasn't giving them and eventually they stopped. I also only have few memories of this abuse and so there may have been much more to it than I recount here. I don't know why I wasn't just destroyed totally by all of the different types of abuse done to me but I like to think that I was born with some protection around me that to this day I still feel. My higher self is too developed to give in to this dark and evil side and so I tend to remain a lone yogi because evil leaves me be and there are so few of us left.

At the time this was happening there was, as has been revealed since, a programme of mind control running covertly by certain factions. This was carried on after the war by those who had been experimenting on prisoners of war and were then still operating with the consent of governments. It is referred to as 'Project MK

Ultra' and was run by the CIA in America and it is believed also in the UK. Certainly you can research this subject as there is much information now online.

Healing ritual abuse

This most cruel of mind control methods is used against children. As the saying goes 'Give me a child until seven and I will give you the man'. So getting to children en-masse, is a valuable tool for controlling a population.

As a child, being a witness to ritual deaths is something no child should ever have to experience. In war such atrocities occur where children see such death on a huge scale and are scarred for life with PTSD. The survivors of SRA and Ritual Abuse see such things daily and the war is the control of your mind. Because if you have control of a child's mind you can direct its future, and en-masse, direct a country or even the world.

You become anaesthetised to seeing such horror and put it to the recess of your mind but it is still there. You are made to do all sorts of degrading things that no child should ever be asked to do and eventually the you that you were born as disappears and the sad, empty husk of a person they create takes over.

I had a full life but I never inhabited it. I was never fully present. I did a presentation once and a therapist came up and told me I wasn't in my body. I was a bit offended by this but I see now that she was right. I never fully inhabited my body. It seemed that it was inhabited by many other beings while I looked sheepishly on from the outside. Spending so much of my life outside my body seemed safer because I spent the whole of my childhood living that way.

My world has been one where I didn't exist. I was invisible, just an ugly, pointless individual that no one liked. Whatever I did, however marvellous, was not for me. I wasn't allowed joy. I gave all my joy to my mother and lived my whole life as if I were her because I didn't know who I was. My self esteem was always low and it is that which I had to repair in order to start to de-

130

programme all the bad stuff I had been infected with. The mind control can't survive in a healthy mind. It needs a degraded, ugly, weak mind to be its host.

De-programming

It is very difficult to find a trustworthy therapist to help you with Satanic Ritual Abuse (SRA) and Ritual Abuse (RA) as so many are used to hearing about Child Sexual Abuse (CSA) but when it comes to disclosing this stuff it can freak them out. I was lucky that I had a therapist who didn't reject what I was saying but, at the same time, her knowledge of this subject was limited and so I had to do most of the work myself. I am also slightly suspect that she may also have blocked my progress in not probing deeper about this subject but I still felt she helped me.

Please only do this work if you feel you are strong enough or have support. You may feel you have no option but to go ahead because you want to progress.

The value of a safe, familiar place in which to work with yourself is a valuable tool to have on your progress. The work you do in this place is personal and, if you need to, get a lockable box or cabinet to put your writing in when you have finished.

In this place that you choose for your healing, place any objects in it that you need in order to make you feel supported. This will be personal to you. You should feel comfortable and supported by this environment.

Before you start writing, mentally acknowledge the work that you are about to do. It is very special, this work, because you are meeting with your self for the first time. This inner child has been a stranger to you who has kept you going all your life. There will also be many other inner children to meet who will hold many memories too unbearable to speak of. Talk to each one as if they were a real child needing your care and understanding.

Start a dialogue with this child telling them, oh so gently, that you would like to talk to them. Allow time for the answer and let the conversation flow. You may feel very tired after this so look after yourself. When you feel the conversation is coming to an end, thank them and ask them if you can talk to them again, promising them you will be there for them should they wish to talk. I often found that one child would talk and then finish and another would then take over. Sometimes I would have several all talking, sometimes one on top of the other.

Don't be afraid of this dialogue because you are only talking to yourself and the inner wounded children inside of you need to talk. The conversation is not from anything outside of yourself and is purely done on paper using your unconscious.

At the end of my years dialogue with these split off parts of me I found I had 36 distinct personalities, all with names, memories and personalities. I was never afraid of them as I knew they were part of me and I was so happy to become whole again and also to have verified the memories I had which needed some explanation.

Because my therapist was not skilled in SRA I think I shut the door on it and left it at the point where perhaps I could have gone further.

Having flashbacks to SRA can be quite scary so remember to ground yourself if you get overwhelmed. See my section on 'Grounding' in this book.

Self-esteem

The greatest gift you can give yourself and the only way to heal is to start to love yourself. If you do not love yourself your abusers have won. I can't tell you how to love yourself because you have to find your own way to do that and sometimes time is the only healer. I can only advise you.

You love yourself by stopping any self abuse whatever that is, be it food, self harm, neglecting your body and mind, masturbation, or sex. You know what it is you do to yourself and you have to become consciously aware of that abuse and make a pact with yourself to stop doing it.

When I first had thoughts of self-harm I sat on my hands for two hours until it passed. I still found ways to abuse myself and it takes a lot of will power to stop. I always find thinking of myself as a small child helps me or putting a picture of her in front of me. I don't want to abuse a child so why would I abuse her.

You should also not feel guilty that you do abuse yourself, because you do it to take away your pain but it doesn't last and you have to keep repeating it. The only way out of it is to create a new habit but this time a good one to take away the bad habit. My bad habits were food and being busy, so busy that I exhausted myself.

Once I took away my most obvious coping device I began to feel uncomfortable, bored and fed up. Over time, with no avenues of hiding from my pain, I surrendered and started to become more content.

The boredom I felt and the boring person I felt I had become in doing so eventually waned and I stopped worrying what others would think of me. I had presented a false front for so long that I couldn't hold it together any longer. I started to accept my life as it was, a simple life, but one with less stress and room to heal. The dramas of the stressful life I had had were removed and now I had to confront myself fully. I began to know myself on a different level and started to feel more human and alive. Another plateau in my healing journey had begun.

Understanding My Family

There is so much I could write about Ritual Abuse but it may be too much to write here because I only want to share small chunks of my story to give you a flavour. One thing that healing and researching this subject has given me is an understanding of my own family.

They who abused me in horrific ways were also victims of this 'trans-generational ritual mind control abuse' and were also subjects of it. They would also have been subject to the same treatment as me, where their minds would have been split into a

133

thousand parts. I only feel love for them. Any hatred of them would do me no favours and I refuse to be eaten away by it and become one of them. This family abuse line stops with me.

I had a memory which used to haunt me of my mother sitting in a wooden chair, bound and gagged and looking at me lovingly and scared and crying at the same time. This memory was strange because I never saw my mother naked and don't remember her looking at me lovingly, like a normal mother. So when I started to get flashbacks I realised what that memory was and I saw the whole scenario in full.

My mother who had tortured and abused me had also been tortured and abused as well. All her maternal instincts had been removed and she too had been mind controlled and split into many parts. The mother I knew was not in fact my mother but a shell of a being, trying her best and not realising, like I did, that her childhood and motherhood had been taken away from her. She was not aware of who she was even though she would tell me of the awful way her mother treated her. She even denied that that was true as she got older.

Both my mother and myself had taken from us the chance to be normal, to be a loving family. Instead my family to this day are nothing but zombies and robots living in a make believe reality of happy families. I was lucky I escaped, I am awake but that also has its drawbacks because I now live outside the web that was created to keep me bound and so I live as a maverick, a misfit and outside of society. I would never and could never go back now.

If you have found out that you were ritually abused and no one believes you, you are wrong because I BELIEVE YOU!

The unborn child

The little girl I never had,
alive in my mind,
not in womb.
An empty cradle,
never rocked,
no golden locks,
to comb with silver brush.
So soft to touch skin,
I will never feel,
or love,
or hug,
or hold.
Grow old
without someone to care or behold.
No school days,
or books to read.
No teenage years,
to wrangle with.
No wedding to attend.
No funeral at the end.
I kept her safe.
This child of mine
is the unborn kind.

Alice Little

Dissociating and Splitting

'You have to make a pact with yourself to be present, not to split, that's what they want, don't give it to them'.
Alice Little

My mind has gone into a suspended state where I feel I am in a cocoon protected from the trauma I am reliving at any present moment. This state, which has a slightly euphoric feeling to it, is highly addictive and dangerous. Going into this state as an adult leaves me vulnerable but I can see how it helped me cope with the abuse of my childhood. Now I must make a pact to stop splitting and it is an addiction that is hard to break.

Hold me tight but don't love me

The tight holding of a child is not always easy to observe even when it's happening in front of you. This technique is used in children's homes and mental institutions and by parents who get angry with their children. It is a form of child abuse and is always about control, the child being controlled by the adult who is unable to contain their own anger at a small child who will not do as they are told. The child may be suffering from neglect, abuse and or mental problems by those outside or even by the parent who is holding them.

If done for a long period the child will eventually quieten and split, sometimes they get even more aggressive but in the end the parent or carer must win and so the child splits and disassociates from the situation and may never even remember it.

I remember such a lot about being held too tight in my childhood and still today it gives me claustrophobia if I think about it. In the past the theory was to wrap babies in tight clothes which was called swaddling. This was supposed to keep the baby calm and quiet and I wonder even now if this early tight holding creates splitting.

136

The appearance of the baby after swaddling is quiet and the theory is because it is similar to that of the baby being in the womb it comforts them. But the baby is not in the womb now and it is free of that constricting place. To say that a baby is comfortable in a womb is a supposition and not a fact because no one is able to ask the baby.

When babies cry it's because they are suffering, they suffer because they are a baby.

Contemplation

The birth of a baby is a miracle and much magic is attached to this event, yet rarely is it investigated from the baby's point of view. The following contemplation is my own but inspired from teachings I had from a Tibetan Buddhist teacher, together with my own experience of remembering my birth and conception.

Death and re-birth

Imagine that you have just died.

You have left everything behind including your beloved body. On this journey you are able to take nothing, death has stolen it all. This profound grief at loosing all that you loved, family, friends, home, country and your body have been taken from you. You die alone even though you may be surrounded by many who love you, it is a journey you must walk by yourself.

If you believe in re-birth then the natural conclusion to that would be that the baby you see being born is in fact someone who had just died. Not only have they just died but now they have to go through the pain and suffering of birth. If you don't believe in re-birth it is still hard to deny that the baby feels no pain or suffering.

137

Imagine you are a baby in a womb.

You have no words to describe what is happening to you so your experience can not be explained but only felt. You are now in a womb having gone through the traumatic experience of having died and lost everything. You do not remember who you are or where you are or what you are.

In this womb you will experience many changes and because you are part of this woman, your mother's body, you get to experience everything that she does, only magnified. When she moves, you move. And when she feels, you feel.

You are trapped in this dark womb where you will grow until the time of your birth when your body will be turned around and pushed towards the cervix. Squeezed through this small opening both your mother and you experience great pain and suffering.

When you are born your delicate skin is cleaned without a thought for your feelings, your lungs take their first breath and the beginning of your life of suffering starts. You cry so much because you suffer, suffer from the loss of dying and losing everything and now the pain of re-birth for which you have no words yet.

The only thing you can do is cry and your crying irritates your already worn out parents. No one thinks of you as a human and until you can walk you will be seen as a creature, an alien, different just as the elderly are looked on as another species.

You have started another round of life as this tiny dependant baby.

Now you are an adult it is your responsibility to take care of this child, you, yours alone. So you should make a pact with yourself that from this day on you will not abuse or neglect this vulnerable little thing. Instead you will care for, nurture, feed, clothe and educate this citizen of the world to be of value to the society it is in.

The next time you hear a baby cry don't be irritated, instead look at the incidence of it's birth and re-birth and have compassion for it. After all its just another you.

138

My parent's divorce

'Release the need to blame anyone, including yourself. We're all doing the best we can with the understanding, knowledge, and awareness we have'.
Louise Hay

The day that I came to see as the beginning of my downward spiral was the day that my parents decided to get divorced. My father had picked me up from school early which was unusual and so I had an idea that something was wrong. Driving on the way back he told me quite coldly that he and my mother had decided not to live together any more, I didn't understand. I also didn't understand his coldness and now, if I look at the situation, he had told me while driving so that he didn't have to look at me. In being told this way I had a feeling that it wasn't true.

He took me to stay with my mother who had left quite suddenly and was living with my Nan, her mother. I still didn't understand. My mother told me that I had to decide who I wanted to live with and when I asked why she told me that it was in order to keep it out of the court because if it went to court I may be taken away to a children's home. This sounded very serious and scary, I certainly didn't want to go to court. I felt that I could loose both my parents if I didn't make a choice.

The decision I had to make at that time was far too weighty for a child and I couldn't think. My father was very persuasive and would badger me every week. He told me that I had a month to decide. My mother didn't talk about it again, unlike my father, and so she appeared as if she wasn't interested.

Together with my father's persuasion and the fact that she hit me and he didn't and that his mother, my grandmother, was better, the favour went to him. Once I had made the decision, he took me away in his big fancy car, my mother was crying and running after it. He just calmly told me not to look back and that's what I did.

I see now that he had staged the whole thing to create maximum effect on my mother because he didn't really want me or know what to do with me after that. In turn my mother didn't really want me either, she hadn't tried to persuade me to stay with her. When I asked her why she hadn't tried to persuade me to stay with her, later in life, she said it was because she presumed that I would pick her. She had left it to chance and played with my life.

The decision should have been theirs, the burden was too great for me. I had tremendous guilt at making the decision to live with my father and leaving my mother. You would think that leaving a narcissistic mother would have been easy but as with any relationship built on narcissistic abuse the survivor's bond is very strong and I was also denying any abuse my mother had given me.

Those two things, the decision I was forced to make and the driving away in the car, stayed with me as a frozen captured moment. The grief of it didn't go away, the loss of my mother didn't go away but I went away that day, my drop into depression had begun.

He took me away from her to get back at her, that became self evident through time, he never forgave her. He never forgave me also because I was part of her and part of the life he wanted to forget. I felt that in everything about him and how he behaved when he was near me or around me.

Abandoned

'Your inner child work will give you the chance to re-parent yourself, the way you wished it had been'.
Alice Little

We are in a department store and my mother is angry with me as usual and I do not know what it is I have done wrong. She shouts at me and tells me to 'get out of her sight' so I walk behind her watching the back of her raincoat absolutely terrified. Just to instil more terror in me she looks back at me glaring and I feel rooted to the spot. I split in my mind and go stiff and disorientated. I do not know that she has carried on walking or that she has either left me or doesn't care. When I come out of my stupor I see that she has gone and I cry my eyes out and wander looking for her but she is no where to be seen. I am lucky that someone helps me and I am taken to a room where a call is put out for my mother over the store's loud speaker system. She eventually comes and I don't know whether to be pleased or not because when she gets me on my own I will be beaten severely.

Contemplation on being a small child

You know what it is like to be an adult and how difficult life can be for you, the responsibilities and the worries. Imagine how much scarier it is for a child. This contemplation helps you to be aware of what it was like for you as a child and how you were vulnerable and not responsible for abuse that happened to you. It will also help you to understand yourself by looking at other children and wondering what life is like for them because it is often easier to see the suffering of others rather than yourself. Eventually it will give you compassion for that child that lived through it all.

Contemplation

This contemplation is based on a child's experience of being raised by a narcissistic abusive parent. There are many scenarios and different types of abusive parents so this is a generalisation.

Compared to the adult next to you you are barely able to reach their knees. If you are standing up you have to stretch your neck to see their face. In a crowded street compared to all the adults around it looks like a large and scary place. If the parent or carer you are with is unkind or cruel you will be scared before you even leave your home and feel unprotected when you are out.

Your mind is undeveloped and your vocabulary is limited yet adults will still expect you to understand as if you were an adult with the same capabilities as an adult and get frustrated if you don't. When they hit you because you didn't understand you will not realise that and will cry further bringing more outrage.

Your parents are already angry, frustrated and impatient and anything you do makes it worse. If you ask for something they get annoyed. If you cry because you are in pain they will grab you harshly and try to stop you from crying.

If you want to walk or run around freely it means they have to watch you and they only want to watch themselves. If they see you having fun they will stop you. They feed off seeing you being shamed by being clumsy and falling. They play tricks on you and shock you to see you cry.

You are totally confused because you are afraid and do not want to be punished but you do not know what these parents want. You try to please them but it is impossible. Eventually you go into a world of your own and become a child that no one likes or you act out and become aggressive.

If your parents then hold you and speak to you nicely, especially in front of others you will be even further confused because you do not know if your mother is good or bad. Your well-being depends on these people and in order to survive you have to split them in two to create a bad parent, which you hide in the recesses

142

of your mind, and the good parent which you create in a state of denial and keep to the front of your mind.

Once you start school you will already have started with a learning disability due to the stress of just living with your parents. You will be distracted, be called a dreamer, have difficulty learning and be unable to stand up to the kids and the teachers at school who bully you because you have already been set up by your bullying parents.

At that young age you would not have known that your parents had a personality disorder. You would have thought that you were mad, bad and evil not knowing that in fact, it was your parent's madness that was taking you further and further away from your true self and into a sick and adapted person of their creation.

Your one piece of armour that you have and that they did not expect is that one day you would wake up and realise that you were the only sane person in the family. This is where you are now, waking up, being reborn, getting back to your true self, the person you were meant to be before they tried to destroy you.

That tiny child lived through so much and now its time it had someone on its side – YOU!.

My grandmother's house

So much happened in that house
Big things,
little things,
containing my memories.
A place where I remember,
can see my past.
There are pictures in my mind
of the life I lived there,
where in other houses,
there are none.
Just blankness.
In this house,
of my beloved grandmother,
I ran
and played
and laughed.
I still live there in a way.
But it was a house
where my mother was not
and so
it contains,
also my sadness
and loneliness
and pain.
I must leave it,
one day.

Alice Little

My father doesn't want me

'I've learned that people will forget what you said, people will forget what you did, but people will never forget how you made them feel'.
Maya Angelou

It was a grey day when my father drove me to my grandmother's house with my small suitcase, a grey day indeed. I loved my grandmother but now I was being taken to live with her permanently, I didn't know what I had done. I had heard them talking about me before, my grandmother had said that she was a bit old now for looking after me but thought I would be company for her. I didn't know what they were talking about but eventually I did. I had chosen to live with my father over my mother and now here he was dumping me off. He had a new life now, a bachelor life with his new love, my stepmother, and I was in the way. He planned things, my father, and then didn't explain when or after he executed them. He just bluntly told you what was happening with no explanation, he was a coward. When he left me there and drove off I have a blank space where my mind closed off from the pain of being abandoned by both parents. I was even alone, although with my beloved grandmother, and nobody could make this pain go away.

The suppression that was happening was being compounded because now I was living with my grandmother I felt so alone. I would cry every night and also during the day, but the nights were the worst. I would lie in this big bed in a big bedroom and was too afraid to turn the light off.

My grandmother who had been my rock was not used to the tragic little girl she now saw. She had been brought up in an era where children behaved and crying was a bad behaviour, one which was ignored and not dealt with. It was to be a pattern repeated by the adults in my life.

I learned to hide my feelings and pretend I was OK and I heard them say how well I was dealing with it all, but I wasn't. When he eventually took me back to live with him it was even worse because now I was having to integrate into a step family that didn't want me. My father's indifference to me continued and I grew further and further away from myself and into depression.

In a way I had ignored my father's indifference to me and it wasn't until we became this new family unit that I started to notice it as it really was. Once my stepmother had moved in with her son I was now completely and utterly invisible to him. He gave me no affection other than the inappropriate touch he used when abusing me.

I began to be very needy and hungry for his love and it left a big hole in me that was never filled and always present. It didn't change or get better even when I left home, in fact that made it even worse because then he wouldn't call me or visit or give any support whatsoever. I was ostracised.

My stepmother complained that her and my dad never got any privacy so I spent most of my time in my room but then I got told off for doing that. Both of them hated me and worked together on suppressing me and destroying my self confidence.

Her

She didn't have a mother
HER
she had left
to live with her brother
HER
Now she was
'the other'
HER
Left alone to fend,
misery without end.
HER
Lost child
with no parents.
HER
Was she an orphan,
an alien?
HER
Perhaps a virgin birth.
She got fed up with waiting
HER
and got
the next train.
SHE DID

Alice Little

STEPMOTHER

"Bring me the axe!"
'Mommie Dearest' film script

She stands next to me, this monster dishing out hot mashed potato. To anyone else, a normal family event, but this monster uses such times to abuse and she uses food. Because I am so very afraid of her I do anything to please her to avoid her anger. This game that she plays every Sunday is in order to increase my food intake. Each week she makes me eat more and more scoops of mashed potato until in the end I have a plate with ten scoops which is piled up so high that I could be sick. When she scoops the potato onto my plate and I say yes, she smiles and is pleased with me and because I can never please her I play her game, I dare not leave the food in front of me. My mother used to forget to feed me but this one does the opposite, same thing different end of the scale.

My father re-married within a few years of the divorce. I think he had already known her for some time, very well.

In order to get us to meet he didn't do it properly instead he engineered a meeting with her and her son one day in a café. A chance meeting or so it seemed. He saw her seated nearby and suggested we go and join them. Something inside me had an awful feeling of doom. Perhaps I knew on an inner level that he was being sly, I didn't want to meet these people.

My dad had already decided that we would so that day I was led reluctantly over to meet her and her son. If only he had talked to me about it and had the guts to take me to see them naturally. I think that he didn't want his family to know either, otherwise why keep it a secret? It seems to me now that my father was unable to speak directly about anything which might affect me emotionally, instead he did things in a roundabout way which in the end only made matters worse.

They sent us off, her son and I, to play on the slot machines and we left them to cement their relationship and plot the next step. A beginning which reeked of subterfuge and lies and didn't bode well for the future. I knew in my bones that something wasn't right and I was soon to find out what.

I don't remember what my dad's family said about her but I knew that she was his girlfriend. In a way I had made her into this princess who was going to make my life all right again. But she didn't, she made it worse. My mother, the narcissist, had left my life only to be replaced by another, equally unkind, but this time a stranger and even more scary. Deeper and deeper into the darkness I went.

The day she moved in I realized with a finality that my mother was never coming back and that this was to be my life. No one talked to me about it, it just happened. I hid in my room and cried, I didn't know they could hear me. I cried for the loss of my mother and also for the unknown ahead of me which no one had explained.

Instead of being comforted or being understood my father dealt with it very cruelly. He burst into my room and told me to stop crying and that I had upset my stepmother. Then he told me he was going to send her in and I was to say sorry to her and that from that day on I was to call her mother. She came in and I hugged her and said sorry for upsetting her but I knew it wasn't right and I lost all hope. It was the last time we ever hugged. I was now alone without comfort and support, all my avenues were blocked and I felt trapped and lonely and very unhappy.

That day I took a breath in and out and found it hard to breath in again. I felt suspended and unreal and very afraid. I retreated more and more within myself. I had cried for years unheard and now here I was being told not to cry, so I did, I was too afraid to.

There was a semblance of family life, a sort of pretend happy family story that we wore for others. But behind the scenes my stepmother's hatred of me was vicious, cruel and spiteful.

I was so unsure of myself by now and I was running on empty and that gave her the ammunition to tear me down whenever she could. I was utterly afraid of her. I didn't recognize the gentle spoken sweet lady that appeared when we went to visit relatives because I never saw that side of her, ever.

By the time I had started work I was bad with my nerves, terrified of displeasing her. I went to the doctor who put me on antidepressants which only made me sleepy and she told me that pills won't help anyway and that it was up to me. I can't imagine a doctor saying that now. In a way I'm glad she did but also not glad because I needed help really and had found none. Yet telling me the pills won't work perhaps stopped me from getting hooked on them or having the terrible side effects that these drugs have.

Two other things happened that drove me deeper and that was that my stepmother was pregnant and so was my mother. My mother now had a new life and family and so did my dad but I belonged to neither. I was just a ghost from the past. My brother was born very shortly after and I had to look after him. He was a lovely boy and although I found it stressful to look after him I now had someone to hold and love. My stepbrother was sweet too but it didn't take long for my stepmother to turn my siblings against me or at least create allies which were on her side in any disagreement.

I had a longing to live with my mother and unsuccessfully ran away to be with her but each time something happened to stop me. I told her I wanted to live with her but she said that I couldn't do that until I was 16 as my father was my legal guardian. I sort of wonder what the real story was because she could have fought for me but she never did. I was trapped and afraid.

My mother within a year moved away to live in Cornwall, the other end of the country and I felt totally and utterly abandoned.

Ugly day

My ugliness embarrasses me.
I turn away from their gaze,
ashamed of what they might see,
in me
On these days,
every pore in my body,
becomes a mass of putrid purple,
that festers in my soul.
Crying out for love,
but finding only hatred
in their eyes,
disgust in their false smiles.
I see me as they see me,
as she saw me long ago,
I carry it like a bad smell,
because that is who I am,
some days,
ugly days.

Alice Little

Puberty, time for more cruelty

'You're just a long streak of misery'.
My stepmother

My stepmother's narcissism seemed to get worse by the day. She was always angry and nothing I did was ever right. I was moving into my teens and she did everything she could to make me look as unattractive as I was feeling.

I was starting to grow breasts and pubic hair. I was gangly and unsure and, worst of all, I had to have a bath with my brother, six years younger than me. My stepmother would be washing him at one end while I cowered ashamed at the other trying to hide my body by hunching over. The idea of this charade was to save money by using less water but my family weren't trying to save energy or the planet, they were abusive and mean. My father was able to afford new cars, a garage and to run these cars and that, in itself, was a big expense. Hardly anyone in our street or town owned a car. It's hard to imagine I know but it's true.

I started to strap my breasts with scarves under my clothes so that no one would see them. I used my father's razor to shave off my pubic hair only to find that when they grew back it was very painful and itchy. I wonder that my stepmother didn't notice what I had done but she probably did and would have enjoyed my shame.

Eventually I could stand it no more and asked my stepmother if I could bath alone. Asking her for anything was an invitation to anger. Her words were not kind and she was furious so she said I could but that I would have to get in the bath after my brother using his dirty water. Getting into that bath of dirty water, with the scum from a bar of soap floating on the top, was as bad as bathing with my brother. She had got me again. The shame of my newly growing woman's body was impounded but she hadn't finished with me yet.

Cruelty is not something that I have in my nature and if it was or I were to find it within me I would confront it and weed it out.

152

Not harming others has been my main premise for living but my stepmother's personality was such that whenever she could harm, she would. My brother was regularly beaten by her and to get her attention he would goad her.

At the same time I was being bullied in the area that I lived in, by both children and adults. I wondered afterwards if perhaps it was a campaign set up by my step mother. When I walked past adults they would whisper about me and some would be downright rude. Children would come up to me and call me names and throw stones most days. If I had a go back the parents would stop by and tell my stepmother I had shouted at their kids and she would believe them and then she would have a go at me. Often I would be made to go and apologise for something I hadn't done or hadn't started. It didn't make sense but now I realise that I was so bullied at home and felt so unsure of myself that others would see that in me and pick on me.

My first period

I didn't know what had happened to me when I started to bleed while outside playing on my bike, I was eleven years old. I was scared to go inside and tell my stepmother because I knew that she would shout at me for ruining my clothes and I was right.

She didn't tell me what was happening to me or why. All she said is you need to keep away from boys now. The only form of help for periods then was sanitary towels and you needed a belt to hold them up. No simple sticky strips like they have now or Tampax and the pads were so very thick that most people referred to them as a loaf of bread.

My stepmother gave me a sanitary towel and I had to put it between my legs without a belt to hold it just a few safety pins. She said she would ask my aunty for one of her old belts. I don't know why she didn't buy me one or give me one of her own but I do know that I was shamed by it all. When I got a belt from my aunty the elastic had gone and it was too large, making the sanitary towel slip down from my knickers.

She limited the amount of sanitary towels she gave me which meant I had to wear the same one all day and it stank. I would wrap toilet paper round it and put masses of talcum powder on it. To compound it all I had to bring the towel wrapped in paper and put it on the fire. She would always move it around with a poker until, shame of shame, my bloodied towel could be seen by all.

I learned to be ashamed of my body and ashamed of the way I looked and any way she could make this worse for me she did. I felt that my presence disgusted her and so I stayed in my room as much as possible but then she would tell me off for being in my room.

Breasts

My breasts were growing and I was embarrassed but I wasn't given a bra. Instead I had to ask her for one, which as usual provoked anger. It was a real nuisance to her and she didn't want to buy one. So instead she asked my aunty to give me one of her old ones and I had to go around in an old bra that didn't fit at all. How I was perceiving myself through these tender teenage years was becoming worse and worse but she hadn't finished with me on that score.

Hair

I longed for long hair but she felt it was too much trouble and so she cut it very, very, short just like a boy. When I had washed it she would tape my sideboards into curls onto my cheek overnight. In the morning she would pull this off and I would be left with a mark on my cheek that stayed for a long time. The pulling off of the tape was painful and I can now see that all this was done in an act of cruelty to hurt and humiliate me.

Throughout my life my hair had been a burden. Firstly by my mother who always said it was too thin even though the reason for that was living conditions, being abused, stress and not being fed. Then my grandmother didn't like my hair because it wasn't curly so she would spit on her hands and wind it in rags until I looked as if I had an afro and I was so ashamed of it. The teachers

154

complained that my hair was so fine that my ribbons fell out and they were annoyed at putting them back for me. Then as if I didn't hate it enough my stepmother compounds it by her treatment of it too.

Clothes

When I asked for new clothes I was given some clothes by my auntie who was the same age as my stepmother and these clothes were beyond horrible. They were two sizes too large and they were designed for a lady who was not only my stepmother's age but also from a woman who made my stepmother look kind. Whenever I saw this lady she was unkind to me and to wear her ugly dresses made me also feel ugly.

I would eventually get my own back when I started to work as I started to buy my own clothes and was very interested in fashion. I experimented with clothes and would try vintage outfits which looked incredible. My dad, however, thought otherwise and would actually disown me by walking on the other side of the road.

My father, I can see now, colluded in my stepmother's hate of me, they both just laughed at me. I was gangly and unsure of myself and having created this person they then set about kicking me a bit further into shape. Yet I always had a rebellious side they couldn't get at and I think that is why I survived because I could certainly imagine having given up sooner.

There are many seemingly simple hidden and innocuous things that parents do to children in the guise of nurture which are in fact made to put you down. Many parents use words to do this but the things my stepmother did to me were done to make me feel unattractive. From the outside these seemingly innocent things are what make a child feel crazy because if you were to complain about it they would just tell you you were ungrateful.

During this time my father always had money for a new car and clothes and new things for the house even though my stepmother seemed to always be short of money when it came to me. Yet even saying this makes me feel as though I sound spoilt and ungrateful. Such is the gaslighting of the narcissist.

Teenage years are hard to get through for parents and children alike I know but to be just downright cruel, there is no justification.

Death

Who will care
when I die?
Who will weep?
No one,
not a person.
I will die alone,
like a wild animal,
in the forest.
Maggots will eat my flesh
and in years to come,
the stench
of my decaying body,
will alert
strangers to come,
looking at what was me
in disgust.
As they did,
when I lived.
I am a stranger to all,
but most of all
to myself.
I have had many small deaths
ended up alone.
ALONE
ALONE
DEAD

Alice Little

Leaving home

That one sentence from the Beatles song 'She's Leaving Home' is such a descriptive phrase that resonates with me. How you can be at home with your family or with others even in a crowd, yet be alone. How people such as narcissists can make you invisible. Such a clever use of words.

I left home at the age of sixteen when I could legally do so without being dragged back or sent off to some home as a runaway. It felt like a great relief at the time but looking back I can see that I was so damaged by life that being on my own was probably not good for me. I was really running away that day and I spent the rest of my life running and moving and leaving and getting away. It is something that has never left me. I am always on the run.

I already had depression but I didn't know it at the time. I went back to the doctors and all she did was prescribe me Valium tablets. I took them once, fell off some ladders and threw the tablets away. I was never referred to a counsellor or any help, other than tablets, so I struggled on alone and never went back to the doctor again.

I was now living in a bedsit with a shared kitchen and bathroom with one other lady. It was a tiny box room but it was my home for now. My father didn't discuss my leaving at all and as usual, he pretended it all wasn't happening. He did come to see me when I first moved in and told me that I was crazy. That was his support. Even though I told him I couldn't stand living with my stepmother he ignored me and promptly told all our family he couldn't understand why I had left home. He played the martyr and I was the rotten, badly behaved daughter, the scapegoat. The rest of the family treated me as if I was a leper. No one ever offered me any help or support.

Not only was I depressed but all the men I met at that time left me for two reasons, one was that I wouldn't have sex with them and the other was that they got fed up with my depression and sad stories. My only friend had troubles of her own and had been manipulated by an older woman who, on the quiet, warned me away from her telling me that she was looking after her now. So we drifted apart a bit.

Then my boyfriend of two years just didn't turn up and gave no explanation. When I tracked him down he said he was sick of hearing my problems. I was devastated. But it was a lucky escape because he was, unknown to me at the time, a pathological liar, a thief and a narcissist. He would enter my life several times and each time he left devastation in his wake until I finally realised what he was, though narcissism at the time was not a word I knew.

I was now on my own, my family didn't bother even calling me they just shunned me. Then my mother called from Cornwall where she was now living and said she wanted me to come and live with her. I made the mistake of going because I had nowhere else to turn to but I regretted it. I was older now and independent and, of course, I had left my job without a means of earning a living and dependant on my mother for a roof over my head. I had some money but not much and I was now installed as a baby sitter for her two children.

It was just by chance that I spoke to my previous employer who said he would love me to come back. So I packed my bags and left Cornwall. My mother never, ever forgave me for going back home and she brought it up frequently.

When I got back home I started my job and tried to be happy but I wasn't. Then out of the blue I was offered a promotion in another town. It was a chance I couldn't miss. Little did I know that being lonely in the town I was in was nothing compared to being lonely in the town I was about to move to.

My Body

Each one of them
a coward
Leaving me standing
alone
waiting
anticipating,
their arrival,
that never comes.
Because I didn't give them
the one thing they wanted.
Not me,
but my body.

Alice Little

The Narcissists I loved

'Everything the Narcissists do to you is built on a fear of that exact same thing happening to them'.
Alice Little

When I moved town at the age of 18 I was totally alone and knew no one. I was living in a grotty bedsit and I was very depressed. My father had gone cold on me and was punishing me for having gone to live with my mother and now my mother wasn't happy that I had left her. I was lost and vulnerable in a strange city and even my job, which had kept me going, now turned out to be nothing like I had been promised. I was working in a strange town with a drunk, dirty old man as a boss. He tried to kiss me several times and when I said no he told me it was my fault because I fancied him.

I tried to keep myself going by dressing up and going into town to shop, it was about a half hour ride. I was looking around a shop when a man came up to me and started to talk to me. He asked me to go for a coffee with him and I went. The people we meet when we are lonely are not the people we would choose when we aren't.

It was the 70's and he asked me what I felt about 'free love'.I had no idea what he was talking about so I was very shocked to find out what he meant. He then asked me if I was a virgin and said that he didn't believe in free love either.

We travelled back and I found out he lived near me, a coincidence. I didn't put two and two together at the time or I would have realised that he had been following me. He was grooming me, though I didn't know it at the time. I had been set up for grooming as a child and it just carried on. The problem was, and is, that if you have been abused and groomed as a child you have no idea that you can say no to anyone. You are not aware that you are being groomed. Who better to groom than a pretty young girl on their own who has no friends and who's parents don't care.

During this time I introduced my mother to him. I was waiting for her to tell me he was totally unsuitable for me but she said nothing. I was a bit surprised because he was a lot older than me and subconsciously I knew he wasn't right. I never told her about what really went on.

So we saw each other several times, I met his friends and as usual I had ended up with someone I wasn't into, it just happened. When he started to get possessive with me and getting more insistent about having sex I ended it, but he hadn't.

He stalked me for months sending flowers, cards etc. and would come at 5am in the morning knocking on my window, I was terrified. Then he would wait until I walked to work and follow me until I had to walk a long way out of my way to get to a bus to work. One day he just came right up to the gate as I was leaving for work and started to have a go at me, then he hit me.

That was a big mistake on his part because it's not something I would ever tolerate' not then and not now, but I was scared and my nerves were bad.

The final straw came when I saw him as I was on my way home, from the top of a bus, walking towards my house. I knew I was in danger and I knew he wasn't going to let me go. So I got off and went to the police station and asked them to take me home, they refused but I insisted as somehow I had heard that you had a right to ask for this at the time.

The police man was young and I told him what had happened. We caught up with him and the policeman got out of the car and talked to him while I sat there. He walked past my window before the policeman got in the car and said, "I didn't think you would take it this far"! The policeman got in and said that he seemed like a nice man. I knew then that I would have to move, a move which would be one of many in the next ten years. I was very badly affected by this incident and my nerves were shot. This affected me for many, many years afterwards and was compounded by the events that followed, none of them good.

My first husband

During the same time that this was happening I met the man, who years later, was to become my first husband. He was a friend at first but later in life I realised that he was just like all the other men I was to meet, he didn't care about me either. He was a constant in my life, a raft I clung to in a turbulent ocean and someone who I turned to when things got bad, but it wasn't right. He was a substitute for my parents who didn't care. His parents were also a substitute for the home life I never had, but they too would try to mould me and shape me into what they wanted.

I didn't realise he was also grooming me and using my vulnerability to get to me. Narcissists can also appear as saviours when no one else cares, they appear to care. These are the kind of no good narcissists you meet when your self esteem is low and you have no support.

Both my parents and all of my family's attitude was that if I wanted to move away from home I would have to sort myself out. So that is what I learned to do. I became very independent and self sufficient and I may have stayed on my own but this man, my friend and first husband to be, who I was to spend the next 15 years of my life with, was playing the brave knight. I was so much in need of someone to depend upon that I stayed and stayed until it was too difficult to extricate myself.

I told him about the man who was stalking me and it was he who helped me move. I had to move miles away to find a place to rent and it was very disruptive and debilitating. I had left an abusive home life and had complex post traumatic stress disorder but was not aware of that. All the things that happened after this event were just a series of bad stories that drove me further and further into the madness of depression.

My future husband was there at a time when I needed a friend. That was all I wanted but he wanted more and he engineered a holiday with another couple where I was to stay in a room with her and he in a room with his mate. I wouldn't have gone if I had known it would be other wise, he had set it all up. The first few days the girl was very off and frosty with me and told me in no uncertain terms 'why don't you sleep in your friend's room?' My friend eventually persuaded me to do this and I was quite unhappy about it but he had used the fact of my kind nature to make me feel that I was being unfair.

What happened then was that he persuaded me to have sex when I didn't want to. It made me feel sick. Its hard to understand if you haven't been sexually abused and groomed as a child to know how that could happen, why you didn't say no. I feel ashamed just thinking about it. He was incapable of having sex, it didn't work, never the less he constantly tried, among other gross things he did to my body which made my flesh crawl. Over the years I eventually stopped the sex. It was too awful and strangely enough he eventually stopped trying.

As the years went on this man, who had nothing when I met him, with my support, became very wealthy. Our life style was full and rich, We went to the best restaurants and travelled in style. Here I was, a girl from poverty tasting another side of life. I did everything for him so that he could work unstressed and relax at the end of the day and at the same time my career was doing well. He tried to get me to stop work once he was earning good money, but I wasn't going to do that, I was much too independent.

I didn't notice it when he put me down about my looks or my dress because it was how I felt about myself. I also didn't notice that I had become his slave, though others pointed it out. When the two of us went out for dinner he didn't talk to me. He didn't talk to me when he came home from work either as he said he had talked enough all day.

I ignored the put downs about how I had arranged the food on the plate or how I had cooked it. I ignored how he told me I was fat when I was slim or that I looked old when I was young. His remarks about my scrawny rats tail hair and footballer's legs I laughed off but the slow drips went in until I felt I actually was who he was telling me.

I felt his hatred of me beyond the fancy holidays and presents, it's just that I didn't believe it. He started a new job which I knew instinctively was a death knell for our relationship when I heard how it was run for singletons. When he corrected me about the way I was dressed when I met him from work, I would often stop off and buy new clothes before meeting him. Then he stopped me from meeting him, making me stay in the car so no one would see me. I didn't meet with the criteria of the woman he wanted to be seen with in his new world. Money was corrupting him.

Then he would stay out late with young women from his workplace who would drape themselves around him openly and talk about the presents he gave them and thanked him for the meal. If I look back now I see that these young girls were bait for clients and may even have been hookers employed by the company.

During this time I was deeply looking at the effect of my childhood abuse and I struggled to keep it together, yet I did. I kept on working and I kept on pretending.

One day I spoke to my husband and told him we need to talk about our relationship because it's not working. I suggested going to a counsellor together but he ignored that suggestion so I told him that our relationship was on the rocks and I was thinking of leaving.

Nothing happened so I told him I was looking for a flat but still he ignored me. I found a flat and rented it yet I still found I couldn't leave. Then one night when he was out, as he was every night, I had had enough. I drunk a bottle of wine and was sick and I knew then that I was leaving.

When I did leave he came after me, saying that he didn't believe I would go. He took me for meals and was charming for the first time in years, but it was too late. Then one night he came to pick me up from my grotty rented flat which had no furniture, in a very expensive car. It made my blood boil that he could do that, here I was with nothing and he was flaunting his wealth, like I would be impressed.

It was that night that I said to him there was no going back and he would have to help me out with some money. He told me that he would only give me £10,000 which I stupidly thought seemed a lot. How stupid I was! We had combined assets, houses worth a lot of money and I had my name on the deeds but had stopped paying the mortgage.

I went to a solicitor who advised me I would need a house to live in, we had several, a car, I had one which I had bought myself, and a pension, he had several. I wasn't bothered about being rich, in a way it was never me, I just wanted enough to live and move on with my life. So that is what I thought I would get. Then I went to see my solicitor again who informed me that my husband had spoken to her and I should just take the money that he had offered me.

I had ignored a conversation that I had had with him about some thugs he had used to help him sort things out. I didn't realise he was intimating future possibilities and he must also have got to my solicitor.

You may wonder why I don't go after him now because a lot of people are doing it and winning historic cases. I no longer want his money. I have just enough to get by on and a roof over my head. Everything I have is my own, I earned it and it is enough.

It is a long time ago since all this happened and I was hurt for a very, very long time. The hurt came from the fact that I had been so kind to him yet, when it came to it, he hit me where he had control within the relationship, money. Money was now his god, he could never get enough. Looking back our relationship was never right from the start. He even told me that all he was looking for was a cook and a cleaner.

The story I have told about this man is only the tip of the iceberg as to what happened during those years but it is enough to give a flavour of what life was like before and after. As I said before, be warned, the people you choose when lonely and needing support, love and friendship are not the ones you would choose if that were not the case. None of the men I met, not one, loved or cared about me. Their only priority and reason to be with me was sex. That is until I met my second husband.

The good thing to come from this whole sorry mess was that I found a man who is everything this man wasn't. He didn't have money but he had everything else, love, kindness, sensitivity, generosity and he was just what I was looking for though I didn't know it. I had put an entry in my journal, 'please send me a gentle man', and I got him. There is a way of living with a gentle, sensitive man which requires a woman to learn skills of patience and understanding, I have learned a lot about myself and he has helped me to be a better person.

His support throughout the years has helped me to be with myself in the most difficult of times and I in turn would do anything for him. We are still together today and love and appreciate each other more than ever.

So, if you are a victim of Narcissistic Abuse and think you will never meet another good man, or you hate all men, it's not true. I had to change something within myself to bring this into my life. I opened my heart even though I had been severely hurt.

Prostitution and inappropriate sex

There comes a time in the life of survivors of abuse when someone opens the door to sex that can take you into a world you wished never existed. I have been very lucky to have, just, escaped such things though have lived within an inch of being caught. There was always something guiding me and warning me away from such situations, yet I could still be naive enough to get burned by ignoring what was going on.

I was at the height of my career when I met this man and about to be given a promotion in a highly regarded company. Meeting him, like all other narcissists, meant that I was about to loose everything yet again.

I was very young, in my twenties, and was just friends with my soon to be first husband, who I described above, still a bit naive. When I went for an interview for a job with this company I was given the position immediately there and then. It made me feel very good about myself. I learned a lot about my job and worked with an interesting bunch of people.

Then one day I was approached by a girl who had befriended me before, asking me if I would talk to a man who also worked for the company and he wanted to meet me. I wasn't to know at the time but I was being groomed by another prostitute for a pimp, him.

Here again I was going along with another man that I wasn't totally interested in so all I can assume is that he was using grooming techniques on me. The first one he used on me was telling me a really sad story about his childhood and of course that's all you have to tell to an empath, a kind person, a sensitive person. I know now that they had watched me for a while to see the signs of not going with the crowd and of low self-esteem. They know who you are and they in turn hide who they are until it's too late.

He lost his job with the company and so I gave him money and helped him to get a flat and a new job which he would loose very soon. I ignored it when he started to tell me how to dress. I ignored it when he took me to clubs where prostitutes and drugs were available.

He was a man into drugs and guns and bad friends and he had a chip on his shoulder. He was probably being used by these men to lure girls like me into a life of drugs and prostitution. He didn't bank on me seeing through this because I woke up very early within the dream because he showed a potential of violence and as I have said earlier, violence is the one thing that only happens once with me.

I had terrible trouble with my nerves due to being afraid of him. He was quite mad and unpredictable. I had no choice but to leave him because he had actually now moved into my flat and I left in the night before he came home. Not only did I loose my flat but I had to give up my job which I loved.

At the same time as this, yet another man entered my life who I thought was just a friend to me. It was nice to just go out and have a meal or a chat and that is all I thought it was. He was the one

168

who helped me to do a midnight escape from my flat, saving me from the hands of the potential pimp I was leaving. I thought this friend was my knight in shining armour helping me at a time I needed it. However this was not to be the case. Watch out for those ones too, the kind ones, looking for a chance to get into your life.

He too had, in fact, groomed me and I ended up having sex with him, although I didn't want to at all, but I did because I felt he had helped me and I couldn't say no. I ended up living with him because I had no where to go. I could have looked for a place to rent but I was so traumatised I couldn't think. It was a mess, I see that, a pattern of behaviour that seemed to be repeating itself time and time again.

My first husband to be was still in my life but we had fallen out. Yet he wouldn't let me go. He kept on trying to persuade me to go back to him and I was in such a mess I cried constantly because I didn't know which way to turn or who to turn to.

Eventually the man I was living with became too possessive and I was never really into the relationship anyway so I left. As usual I had fallen into a relationship, with another set of problems, with my eyes shut.

I didn't know that I was depressed and I didn't know that I had CPTSD due to not only my bad childhood but also the many things that came after it, again and again. I felt that I was lashed to the front of a boat in a great storm that never seemed to abate.

I had had a successful career and now I had to go backwards taking a job eventually that I would never have taken if I were not so desperate. I thought my life had been a success but recounting it now I realise that it was a very sad life and yet with a few amazing happenings. My career was a success and the one constant in my life. It was my coping device when all around me was falling apart it kept me going. Eventually I would claw my way up the career ladder but I had been severely damaged by then.

One day it just had to all fall apart in a big way, it was a storm waiting to happen.

Speech Hypocrisy

There is a hypocrisy to speech,
half truths tumble from our lips,
niceties that we all regurgitate.
Not caring, only wanting,
to hide our true selves.
Sides of laughter and derision,
sides of lamb and beef,
that we keep locked
within our drooling mouths.
Kept in check to pretend we are not
the cannibals we hide.
Eating our words instead,
pleasant and nice outside.
Enjoying those who can spew vitriol.
Longing to be free within speech.
Longing to be ugly.

Alice Little

Talking and communication

"No one puts baby in the corner".
'Dirty Dancing' film script

If you can't talk, how do you communicate, by writing? I mean you can't actually go up to someone with a pad and pen and start a conversation that way. But that's my preferred method of communication, along with dancing, two mediums in which I can find and be truly myself. I can't articulate in the way I would like to, my tongue gets in the way.

Two stumbling blocks from my childhood are that I was taught to be quiet, shut up and make no noise. So I learned to be quiet. I'm not shy, I'm just sometimes anti-social because I really don't want to waste time on my biggest hate, small talk. I don't understand it and it makes me anxious.

Over time I've learned that you have to start with insincere niceties before you can go in with some real deep conversation and I get bored within a minute. I want to know what's in peoples hearts and minds and it takes so long to get there.

My first husband didn't talk to me and I had to be quiet whenever he was driving and when he came home from work. If we went out for dinner he would just sit looking bored, as if he wanted to be somewhere else. At the end of the night he would tell me that I always talked too much when I've had a drink.

Communicating with people is a skill and some people have it but most don't. I rarely find someone who is so comfortable in their own skin that you feel you could just be yourself with.

Now, because I have chosen to go No Contact with my family, (the origin of my misery and abuse), I have developed another communication block. I can't freely talk about who I am because I don't want to create a connection or a link which will lead my family or anyone else from my past back into my life. So I have to watch what I say or give away, which in itself may appear a bit cagey to others.

Now at this moment in time I'm trying to re-create myself to find who I am beyond abuse. Perhaps you are too? Trust is still something that I struggle with no matter how far I have come in my healing. Yet I only have to look at my husband to know that I am lovable and can trust another and that gives me hope.

Slowly I will start to use my skills, the ones I have learned over the years, to start a new beginning, a fresh start and live again in a new way. Writing this all down, these stories from a long ago past, has helped me to let it go. I hope you too will do the same one day. It's not about being a good writer it's just that you have to tell your story, you really do. I hope I'm around to read yours, whoever you are.

The Legacy

'They had to go and leave me something of no value'.
Alice Little

The legacy of Narcissistic Abuse is depression. The narcissist leaves in their wake a destroyed personality, a husk of a being, emptied out and used by their abuser. The narcissist is a sinister character, worse than any depicted in fairy stories of old. In Cinderella the narcissistic family is aptly described. Her mother is dead and her father marries again and now she has a wicked stepmother and her spoilt daughters and Cinderella becomes the scapegoat. The narcissists can only pretend to show beauty while Cinderella has an inner beauty that they are without. This is what the narcissist is trying to take away, this authentic goodness and inner beauty.

As you can see, there were many things that contributed to my depression, compounded it and made it worse but my early parenting and abuse created the seed. If my parents had nurtured me and supported me I may have had a better start. Everything I did in my life I did it myself without any support other than that which I paid for. The only support I have ever had which meant anything was and is the support of my husband.

I am now at a point where depression does not grip me like it used to. I was depressed every day and thought it was how I would always be but that changed. I can still get depressed but I try not to let it take me over. I now see it is happening whereas before I didn't see it happening, I just didn't see anything other than depression. Now I see there is something beyond depression.

With a start like mine I would expect to have some residue of the damage that abuse gave me but I make an effort to live beyond that because I can't afford my abusers to win. Whatever you have in your tool kit you can use it to support you. I use my stubbornness and defiant nature to defeat the depression they created within me because I actually feel the depression is them. They have taken enough of my life from me.

So if all you do is defeat your depression by thinking you are defeating your abusers then you would have attained a great victory.

"Come on depression (abusers) and do your worst because if you want to mess with me your going to get beaten".

You could stay depressed all your life or you could try to be happy. Do we have a choice? I started to become happy about five years after leaving my narcissistic family for good. Once I had gotten over the grief of losing them I realized that I was wasting my time even thinking about them. They had sucked me dry and I had to decide to move on.

When I left my family of narcissists I didn't think it was possible to ever heal from the effects of their abuse but I have. I have found that healing never ends, it just moves into another level, bringing things for you to look at from your past that you can now deal with. When you move on in your healing journey you can decide if you want to look at things from your past or not, sometimes you can just say no, not today, and send them away. Or you are able to look at your history in a more dispassionate way where you are not so swept along by your emotions.

Friends

I wanted you once,
when none were there,
to put a friendly face to,
to be with,
as I was,
dark
and
sad
and
lonely.
You didn't see me
You passed me by
and I was left
as always
to mop up
my own tears.
Now I see you
but it is too late
too much damage
has been done
to my heart,
to let you in.
Now in age
I care not for other
but stay
as always
alone
without.

Alice Little

Grounding

'Be like a tree, head reaching to the sky and the sun but feet
firmly planted in the soil.'
Alice Little

I would consider myself a grounded sort of person so have been able to keep my feet firmly on the ground during the re-surfacing of memories and after. I seem to have a strong inner core that aids me and grounds me and has helped me to survive. Where it comes from I don't know but I think it's because I only had myself to turn to in times of trouble and so I am able to depend on myself when things get tough, sad but true. Nevertheless I still find times when grounding helps.

If you are the sort of person who is not naturally grounded and can get swept away by strong emotions then you will need a set of tools to use when you find yourself overwhelmed.

Grounding tool box

Think about the earth and the colours of the soil you walk on, brown, black and rust. Colours of the earth that you can visualise, wear or carry with you.

If you feel unsafe when walking out should memories surface carry a small earth bag. It could contain earth or a small stone or a symbol that represents the earth and grounding which is personal to you. This is not just 'new agey' nonsense, it is a way to trick your mind into a positive safe and grounded place.

Because I am very grounded I tend to wear a lot of blue which helps me to be more airy and fluid. If you are not grounded then wearing earthy colours will help.

If you have flashbacks while out or are overwhelmed by them at home you will be helped by reminding yourself of where you are right now and that the flashbacks are part of your past and not the present even though it may appear and feel as if they are happening now. If the flashbacks don't stop and you feel unsafe try to get yourself into a place that you can feel protected until they die down.

Ground yourself by:

Telling yourself
- Your name
- Your age
- The date
- The time

My name is ………I am….. years old….today's date is… and the time now is…….

Plant your feet firmly on the ground and breathe naturally and easily to stop hyperventilation and panic attacks.

To help you breath you can do 7/11 breathing which is 7 breaths in and 11 out.

Over time you will find the right way to ground yourself in the present time that is personal to you.

Flashbacks

'Time travellers that's what we are'.
Alice Little

It's hard to believe your flashbacks especially as no one believes you either. They are happening to you for a reason, the reason is because you are waking up and your mind is able to process your past now. You are not going mad, you are becoming sane. Now you can look at your past as it really was, not how you invented it in order to survive because it was bad.

Waking up is never easy but most people never get this opportunity, they stay asleep the whole of their lives, that's an un-lived life. Your flashbacks will keep coming until you listen to them and one day, though it doesn't seem like it now, they will stop. You may get flashbacks in the future but their intensity is not so vibrant.

If you want to go with the flashbacks in order to retrieve memories and process them remember to take care of yourself afterwards because it can be very exhausting. Allow yourself the time and space to recuperate.

Remember if you are overwhelmed:

- It is not happening now
- Keep your eyes open
- Distract yourself by moving or singing
- Ground yourself by saying the date
- Stay grounded
- Give yourself time to recuperate
- There are others who are experiencing this right now.

Conclusion-Mind control

They have a mind of their own but they still want mine it's not for
sale at any price.
Alice Little

In the end the conclusion is that mind control is the sole purpose
of others. So it must be that instead, you take control of your own
mind. When you have been sexually abused a therapist will often
tell you to inhabit your body because you can often spend so
much time dissociating and living outside of your body. I would
say inhabit your mind. Think about it for a moment, which part of
you split, was it your mind or your body? I mean did your body
leave or did you leave your body, if so what left your body?
Whatever you call it, mind, consciousness, it is this which leaves
and it is this that will leave when you die.

When you meet a narcissist his/her sole aim is to get control of
you. If they can't they will move on to someone they can control.
If you have been bitten by the narcissist's poison then you were
already primed to be controlled by them because you had most
likely been conditioned by a carer, adult, school, parent, family or
even friends well before you met them.

The only cure is to train your mind so that the possession that
happens with Narcissistic Abuse can no longer be an option. To
control your own mind to such an extent that the narcissist can no
longer see you and that you will either be immune to them or
aware of them. Where once you may have felt invisible now you
are healthily invisible to the narcissist. While you are still in the
narcissists web you will be vulnerable to other narcissists, male
and female. Once you can really see the narcissist for what they
were rather than the illusion they created, you can move on and
let go.

So how do you train your mind? First you have to get to know
it, to become familiar with it. To become so aware of ego's little
trips that when they happen you can see it. Your awareness of
your mind and its habits will help you to gain strength because

179

you can not always rely on your body to help you. In the end your mind will be your best friend and ally but first you need to slow it down and make it pliable.

Currently you are not in control of your thoughts and mind, you are led like a donkey by anything that involves the five senses. You allow your thoughts to drift and dream but you never pull in the reins and take charge. To do so requires discipline and you may be weak and used to bad habits of thoughts and actions.

Haven't you had enough of suffering yet?

For me I got really, really bored and annoyed with being depressed, of having my life ruined and taken away by lost days of being miserable. Mostly though I felt that staying depressed meant that the narcissistic abusers had won by keeping me down. Healing has to be a decision and time disappears fast. What will you choose.

I chose LIFE!

PART 3

My life as a spiritual journey beyond religion

Thank you

Thank you to all the teachers I met on the way, those from religious traditions and those from none. The teachers who taught me the dance, how to hear the music, use my voice and how to train my troubled mind to heal it and inspire me to love.

Apologies

My explanations in this book of Buddhism and Buddha Dharma are mostly pitiful attempts made by a very dim-witted hopeless student such as myself. So any faults you find in my book are purely due to this. I confess to being a particular bad learner but as my teacher said "sometimes people who are not so intelligent get it immediately". Any Dharma I spout off about in this book are only the words my teacher told me and it's most likely I didn't remember them right, or in the wrong order, or indeed mixed them with my own worldly ideas. My ego disclaims all responsibility for any errors.

The Story of my life and liberation

'There are many layers to waking up and the mind can lie to you telling you you are awake when in fact it's just your ego, come along for the great spiritual ride'.
Alice Little

Where do I begin to tell you the story of my spiritual journey, because trying to find a beginning would be an impossible task.
I have been writing my story in so many ways, yet within it and mainly because of it, there is, intertwined, my spiritual journey.

When I began to write down my story of my spiritual journey I was a bit reticent to do so, it didn't seem right but as I did so I heard my teacher's voice and remembered his words.

" You should write down your story of life and liberation"

This journey is the story of my life because I have always known I was a spiritual being.

In this part I describe, woven within my life story, my spiritual journey. Going from an abusive Christian and Catholic upbringing to trying every religion under the sun. Along the way I tried and trained in so many other therapies, some amazing and some just weird and wacky. Finally becoming a Tibetan Buddhist. Yet even that was taken from me when I went 'No Contact' with my family and my life. Everything I had been practising and learning fell away from me and I was left in a world without spirit, without hope.

Finally coming to a place of peace and acceptance of all the teachings I had been privileged to be given and finding a way to use those teachings in a way shorn of dogma. I found my real self beyond any thoughts or ideas. I had been searching outside myself for that which was always inside, always helping me, I just didn't know that it was part of me.

My healing has come as part of an acceptance of that which is within me, a part that has always guided me and warned me when I listened to it. A part which I also often ignored but which I have now come to trust. It is greater than anything I have ever thought of or could imagine, but I had to first heal and respect and love myself to find it.

This greatness is a birthright which we all have, a jewel we own, and yet we discard it, and replace of a dull piece of coal, a substitute, because we can not stand this greatness within ourselves. We have been taught it is bad to think of ourselves as great, it is always the other person that has the power.

This lie keeps us imprisoned and open to abuse from all those we look up to as leaders, in any area of our lives. My aim is to make this greatness within me grow so that it is a natural part of my life, not separate from it. It is a journey without end that I am still treading.

This was and is my journey!

Thank you for walking it with me.

Alice

We are what we think
from the Dhammapaha

We are what we think.
All that we are arises with our thoughts.
With our thoughts we make the world.
Speak or act with an impure mind
and trouble will follow you,
like the wheel follows the ox
that draws the cart.

We are what we think.
All that we are
arises with our thoughts.
With out thoughts we make the world.
Speak or act with a pure mind
and happiness will follow you,
as your shadow unshakeable.

In this world,
hate never yet dispelled hate.
Only love dispels hate.
This is the Law,
ancient and inexhaustible.

We are what we think.

The Buddha

185

The early years

'Children know this spiritual stuff, adults deny that'.
Alice Little

Before I even began the route of the, so called, spiritual training my family had in store, I had an awareness of a deep spirituality within me. My first memory of this as a very small child is when I stood in the front garden of my home and looking up to the sky I said to myself, "I'm never coming back here", and a voice within replied, "Then you must take everything that happens to you in life as a lesson". I never forgot that voice and throughout my life made it something that I adhered to. Thus finding many reasons why I would not want to come back to this dreadful place I found myself living in.

So with this as a mantra I learned the many lessons that life offered up to me, I just didn't realise that it wouldn't end.

My family were a bunch of Christians and Catholics and within these God-like religions that I was part of, another hidden side emerged. The fine, upstanding church-going families that entered this house of God were secretly worshipping the devil in the form of ritual abuse. The church was nothing more than a cover up to the mind controlling, child abuse, paedophilia cult that I was now part of, within which I was sexually and emotionally abused, sold to others for money and mind controlled by ritual and torture.

While my family upheld a perfect, upstanding, church- going good family disguise I was left to soak up all their hatred as the family scapegoat. Keeping their lies until the day I broke and was unable to keep up appearances any longer. Finally leaving them all and escaping to heal by going No Contact with them all.

This particular part of my life when I was very young was terrifying and even now as I type I feel pains in my body, pains meant to silence me from talking, which of course I ignore. If you have no awareness of ritual abuse it can sound very crazy. They

186

made it up! Invented stories. Watched too many horror movies. But it isn't, it's true and it happened to me.

I continued to go to church until I was about eighteen but had moved town and found that the church was different to that which I had been used to. So I stopped going. Yet I never gave up looking for that elusive something. I decided to explore every kind of religion there was in a search of something that eluded me yet I felt I was looking for. With no luck in finding anything I gave up and carried on with my life, feeling spiritual but following nothing. Helped in my un-spiritualness by my atheist husband.

I had serious depression but I didn't know what to do about it. I was so miserable and my family were no support to me at all and I had to look after myself just as I had done as a child. Yet even though my parents were obviously neglecting me I still blamed myself. I thought if only I tried harder I could get them to give me what they failed to, it was a loosing battle. My loneliness just made my depression worse and so I threw myself into work and tried to block it out.

The Fabergé Egg

They saw you only as a plain egg
'You are not beautiful', they said
So they painted you in lots of different ways
They rubbed you out and started again
But they couldn't paint you good enough for themselves
They got bored with your stubbornness
To not become what they wanted you to be
They got angry
You tried to paint yourself to please themselves
But even you couldn't make yourself
into the beauty they wanted
You got angry with them,
got angry trying.
They threw you to the floor in disgust
the plain shell cracked and inside
revealed a beautiful
Fabergé egg
But it was too late for them to see
That you were the beautiful egg
that they had wanted all along.

Alice Little

Meeting my first husband

'I will always feel sadness for the loss of you'.
Alice Little

When I met my first husband to be, devoid of any family life, I clung to him like a raft from a sinking ship. He became the family I never had and his family became my family and so it made it that much harder to leave. He was a friend and more like a brother so, in a way, it was doomed from the start.

I didn't intend to live with him, I tried to cling to my independence as much as possible but life threw me a curved ball and I had to move from a flat I was renting very quickly and it seemed the only thing to do was to move in with him. I thought it would be temporary but I never left, at least not for a very, very long time. I tried to and even succeeded once, but I went back, unable to cope without him after so long.

I had been living on my own since I was sixteen and now ten years later after moving from one flat or bedsit to another I sort of had a home and some stability. It wasn't what I had planned for myself but it was how it had turned out and so I made the best of it.

My life with him was very full and I lived a life of adventure and wealth but my spiritual side waned and I knew this was happening. I knew if I left him I would grow but I just couldn't leave. When finally I left for my sanity, my spiritual growth started immediately but it was hard to give up the life I had had with him even though it was wrong. It took me a very long time to recover from leaving him, I had no idea it would be so hard. He left me with nothing yet he remained rich, his life didn't change apart from me, everything was the same. He just replaced me for a new model and moved on. When I met him he had nothing and by the time I left he was a millionaire.

I had lived a full life with him yet I was depressed. I had gone from a poor background to being wealthy yet even with all the material comforts I was not content and that felt worse. To be depressed when you're poor anyone could understand and sympathise with that but to have a rich and full life and still be depressed, how do you deal with that?

Then one day I woke up!

I realised that my long term relationship had never been right. I tried to make it work, kept ending it and going back but it didn't change. I suggested we go to counselling to make it work but he didn't see what was wrong with it. His desire for more and more money was taking him into worlds and people that I didn't like and he spent more and more time away from me and with other women.

I think he felt I wasn't good enough for the world he was in now and he let me know that through his emotional abuse and neglect. He took it for granted that I would stay around and I let him treat me like a doormat. I didn't know until long after I left him that I had been abused and used by a Narcissist.

Then I hit rock bottom and I began to have flashbacks to my abusive childhood, a childhood that I had tried to avoid looking at, and my world fell apart. I left the relationship and left my life and everything that was in it. Alone I had nowhere to go to but to look within.

So began another chapter of my life.

Healer

In many shamanistic societies,
if you came to a medicine person
complaining of being
disheartened,
dispirited
or depressed,
they would ask one of four questions.
When did you stop dancing?
When did you stop singing?
When did you stop being enchanted by stories?
When did you stop finding comfort
in the sweet territory of silence?

Gabrielle Roth

The dance of life

'Dance until you can't dance any more, then keep on dancing and go beyond into the stillness that lies within, the movement of the dance'.
Alice Little

When my life totally fell apart I began a journey of self-discovery, looking for the self that had been stamped out of me by everyone around me who had tried to mould me into a shape that was of their desire, none accepting me for who I was. This journey of self discovery took me into many different forms of therapy and self-healing. One of the most significant was dance. I had become very trapped in a self that was very claustrophobic and stilted, I had had the stuffing taken out of me and I didn't know who I was any more, dance changed all that.

Following the beat of the drum

I had looked at many forms of healing and therapy and was in a class learning Shiatsu one day when I heard the sound of drums in a classroom nearby. When it was break time I located where the sound of the drums was coming from. The door was open and people were dancing to the beat of a Djembe drum and as soon as I saw it I thought that's the class I should be in.

The Shiatsu class was a bit dry and boring and the teacher was an older guy with a very pretty young girl as his assistant, who he used for demonstration. The whole process of this type of therapy was much too intimate for my liking and I had my obvious reservations about the guy running it.

So I walked into the dance class and found out when it was held and decided to join that class. It was called Biodanza 'the dance of life' and I stayed for two years.

This type of dancing was just what I needed because I was so shut off from my feeling in both my body and mind. It took a lot of courage because this type of dance included three things, dancing with your self, dancing with another and dancing with a group. All of them were a challenge but I came alive in those classes and it is a time in my life I will always remember with a great fondness.

The music was mostly Brazilian and you either got fired up or ended up crying. When I first joined this group I had no idea I was so shut off from myself. It wasn't until many months later when my teacher got me up to dance in front of a huge class saying at the end, 'you don't know how hard she has had to work to get to this point', that I realised. I didn't know I had changed. I didn't realise that I was now dancing freely whereas when I first started the class I hardly moved. It's just that bad habits can feel normal. Loosing them feels scary.

The first movement in the class that you had to do was dance in a circle holding hands and the circle would weave in and out with the rhythm of the music. You had to engage in eye contact in this dance and it was a scary start. We usually only give ten second eye contact to another and then look away. Beyond that ten seconds it becomes intimate and we are all scared of that. This dance made you realise how you avoided eye contact. I did not realise that I either looked at someone's ear or their lips.

Then you got to experience dancing with another which was equally scary. This was followed by dancing in a group, even scarier for me. Yet though I was scared I still carried on because I loved it, even though at times it was painful. It brought me back to life again.

There was one dance that you did which was called 'The Encounter' and it was beautiful. The music was very poignant and you walked throughout the room meeting another person. You could choose who you encountered and also how you approached another. This meeting may be just a smile, or a hold of hands or even a hug. This was to show you how in real life you can choose how you create your boundaries by showing the other, this is what I want or don't want. Within that dance the other also had to read your signals, so your boundaries had to be non verbal.

In fact Biodanza was a non verbal dance altogether and it suited me fine as talking was something I found difficult having been shut up for so long by my first husband and my family. However, the people were very friendly and we would often meet up afterwards for a very relaxed coffee and a chat or go to another dance in town like Salsa. Good memories of nice people and I have to remind myself that it is possible to encounter such again.

However it seemed that every group I joined there was always one event, one person who dirtied it all. That person just happened to be the man who invented this dance. We were all privileged to be meeting him and he, an elderly man, joined in with the dancing.

In the dance 'Encounter' I walked towards him with my arms open wide and he, in turn, grabbed both my breasts. When I told the lady who was holding the event she, in turn, also grabbed my breast and said 'yes I can see why!' When I look back now I just laugh in disbelief. The one thing that I got from this awful encounter is that I learned to show stronger boundaries with people. The honeymoon period of being in this group waned and I was suffering once again with depression and suicidal thoughts.

However as well as a great healing of self and body and having fun, the work I did on myself made me open to meeting a man I may otherwise never have encountered. He was nothing to do with the dancing but a chance meeting and there he was, my soul mate, my second husband and I am still with him today.

The Goal

There is no goal
Nothing to achieve
Nowhere to go
So, I will stop striving
and instead I will rest
will let go.
Nothing to attain
No place to head for
nothing to do
No boredom in the non doing
I will begin gently to let go
Be in the moment
and that which I have searched for
worked for
sweated tears to attain
will come in its own time
slowly
whenever
it doesn't matter
So I will sit every day
without goal
finding nothing
but myself.

Alice Little

Awakening

'An introduction to the nature of your mind is, when someone who is awake, reminds you about something you already had but forgot. Too near for you to see it was there. Too simple for you to believe it existed.'
Alice Little

My awakening started the day that I admitted to my first husband that I had been abused as a child by a family member. I had told him because I was angry at something he had said and I blurted it out, not really believing my own words. Here was something shameful that I had kept to myself all my life and now I was revealing it to another.

Perhaps it could have been left there as just an awful childhood incident but my mind had seen its chance to open up and open up it did.

There were many things about my childhood that I had never understood and never questioned and now what started to happen was that it all came pushing back into my mind to be looked at. At first I didn't want to look at it all. I had memories of weird stuff that I had ignored and now I started to question what it was all about. Then came the flashbacks.

In a matter of months my whole life had turned upside down and the unhappy childhood I had tried to whitewash came back with a force so big that I thought I would not survive it. My only saving was that I began to trust the process of what was happening to me because I understood that somewhere I was waking up and beyond the awful flashbacks I was becoming sort of whole. I was having a spiritual emergence.

I can understand that my husband would see what was happening to me as strange and he appeared to support me. However he got me to go to a doctor he knew and the doctor wanted me to go to a psychiatrist. My instincts went into overdrive, this was a time when abuse was a taboo subject and I knew this road was not for me.

Then one day I made the mistake of having a drink and I got terrible panic attacks and was arguing with my husband. At that point he told me that I had better get a grip or he would have me locked up. So at that point I kept everything to myself and, being unable to be honest about what I was going through, it got worse. On the outside I hid it very well. As usual I just kept working and working.

For some four years the flashbacks to childhood sexual, ritual, emotional and mind controlling abuse continued and I was exhausted. Everything fell apart. My long term marriage failed miserably as it had never been right to begin with.

Unfortunately I ended up with nothing because he took the money and everything we owned and left me with a mere £10,000. We were very wealthy and I had helped him in his career while also having a career of my own, yet he still left me with nothing as if I had never been with him at all. His life continued exactly as it was only swapping me very quickly for a new model. Meanwhile I was left alone.

I rented a small room with no furniture and was now totally alone knowing no one. All the friends we had known were now just his friends and I had not realised that I had none of my own, having lived my life for him only. I had no contact with my abusive family and now the life I had know literally did not exist.

When you are finally on your own, stripped of everything, you feel a tremendous loss and grief. Here I was, having no contact with my family having admitted my abuse only to be denied and now I had lost my relationship. The only person in the world I knew was a lady who had become my therapist and I was paying for that.

I didn't know how much lower I could get. As a child I had known extreme poverty and horrendous living conditions and now I had gone from a wealthy, busy lifestyle to nothing, absolutely nothing, and it hurt. As well as this I was having to deal with trying to maintain my career while having daily flashbacks. The flashbacks could happen while working, while travelling and in the street. Anything could be a trigger to set it off. Those days were terrifying and I collapsed with vertigo and exhaustion, yet still I kept on working, my only coping device.

We just carry on with our lives don't we, whatever happens to us and that is what I did.

I began to go to workshops and anything that I felt could help me. I started to meet other people but mostly they were as damaged as me, if not worse, and none of them were able to be other than fleeting friends. From a very glamorous life I was now seeing the worst life had to offer. I was a shunned person that no one wanted, someone who if diagnosed would have been seen as having mental health problem. Only I knew that it was in fact a spiritual awakening.

The flashbacks to my childhood sexual abuse abated only to be taken over by memories of the Ritual Abuse I had suffered. Here was something that I had thought was a normal part of my childhood with slivers of memory that I had not really understood and now here it was in full technicolour for me to look at.

That time was hard and terrifying, like watching your own horror movies. I searched for someone who could help me with understanding the ritual abuse and when I found someone eventually she informed me that she would have to now leave the country as people were after her because of her work. I was lost.

My own therapist, who was great, was, none the less, unable to really deal with the stuff I was telling her and after several helpful sessions the memories stopped. I don't know whether it would have helped me to investigate this further but at least I could hold back the dam of horror that was invading my life.

You think it can't get any worse but my mind and soul had other things in mind for me and my next flashbacks were of previous lives. At that point there was no reference for what I was re-living whereas by remembering my childhood sexual and ritual abuse I did have half memories of those times to refer back to and make sense of but this, this was something different.

All I can say about those times is that I totally trusted what I was going through. **I knew it had a purpose.**

Merging

I found one day
myself, cradled in the mind
of the absolute.
Not separate from it,
I was it.
I gazed at the sky
and the clouds.
I soaked up the sun
I, did not exist
That I, could not conceptualise
the feeling of pure bliss
Born again some say
I, who was the I, that day
that felt so merged
Truth is it disappears
only to be found not
in bliss or blue skies
but in the mundane
even in a shoe shop
within the drama of every day life
It follows me now
Just sometimes I don't
realise it is there.

Alice Little

Flashbacks to re-birth and previous lives

'The wound is the place where light enters you'
Jalaluddin Rumi

My first flashback to a previous life was to my pre-conception which happened to me after watching a film in town. The images came boom, boom, boom as I walked towards my car and continued for the whole of the drive home, an hour at least. How I drove back I do not know.

The memory was this:

There is a feeling of great darkness and evil and I am aware of a fall downwards. As I look down I see below me a town, dark and evil with colours of red and black but mostly black. Everything has a feeling of foreboding and misery and I realise I have come back to this place to suffer again. I hear myself thinking the words, "You didn't listen to your teachers words and advice" and I cried and cried feeling a deep despair that I may have had a choice of not returning here. I felt an utter severe pain of failure and despondency.

The image returned again and again and when it stopped I was having panic attacks so bad I thought I was going mad. I was able to call a friend and my husband was supportive but I knew really that neither of them would grasp what I was going through personally. At those moments though it is good to have just a hand to hold. When you are going through something as profound as this it is always best to be careful of who you trust because from the outside it looks like you're very crazy.

Recollection and knowledge of a previous life
My second flashback was when I started to read The Tibetan book of Living and Dying by Sogyal Rinpoche. I had bought this book about a year before I read it. It had just lain on the bookshelf.

Then one day I was advised to look at the book by a Tarot card reader who I had gone to. I was surprised that she would recommend a Buddhist book to me but also surprised that I actually had the book at home.

When I picked it up to read I found that I couldn't understand a word of it. It all looked very intellectual and difficult so I put it down and forgot it. The next time I went to the Tarot card reader she asked me if I had read it and I told her how difficult it had been for me. So she advised looking at the back index and picking out a word and then going back to the page and reading it.

When I got home I picked up the book and did what she advised. Still I found it a bit hard to understand so I leafed through the book and all of a sudden I saw a picture of a teacher who had been Rinpoche's teacher Jamyang Khyentse Chokyi Lhodro and I knew him. I remembered him. It was such a strong feeling that I had to go out for a walk to get away from it. When I was outside I spent the whole of the walk crying so deeply because I knew I had met this man before and I couldn't get the image out of my mind, it was utterly haunting me. The flashbacks to my knowledge of him pounded at my head and I was afraid and didn't know why.

Eventually I allowed this time and this moment to pass and continued to pray in my own way lighting candles and making a little shrine with stones, with no particular following bar perhaps a leaning towards Native American traditions. One day as I sat there looking at the sky I knew I had to find a teacher, that I had gone as far as I could and now I needed a guide. So I prayed strongly 'please send me a teacher'.

It was not long after this that I noticed a retreat being held by Sogyal Rinpoche himself in a magazine and so I decided to go. It was being held in the city and so I travelled down with a small bag and began my spiritual journey which was to last for a very long time.

Flashbacks

I had several other flashbacks to previous lives, all different and all at different times in the past, some as men. I had memories from the moment of birth when I remembered being born together with an older woman who had been hanging around and living off my energy. I felt that this memory was to do with ritual abuse.

It all sounds very wild now as I recount it, but its what happened then. How I remained sane I do not know. There was always a part of me that was shut off from that stuff as if keeping it divided so that I could function. But that was all I was doing, functioning.

It got weirder.

I did a lot of writing when I was recovering from the flashbacks to my childhood and sometimes that writing would trigger things off sometime after I had stopped writing. The next flashbacks I didn't understand at all but I went with them anyway. They were of strange visions of being chased underwater by a long-haired, bearded man and so many other visions that I can't even recount here clearly. Some time later I told them to a friend who told me that they were Greek myths and pointed me towards a book on them. My schooling was not great and we definitely didn't read Greek myths nor did I even know of them or read about them as an adult so I have no idea where the visions came from. I couldn't take any more of these strange memories and so little by little I stopped looking at it all and moved on to another phase of my life. Buddhism.

After all this soul searching I guess it was inevitable that I would turn once again to my search for something spiritual and so next I met my spiritual teacher.

Meeting my teacher

'Then I met you, and rainbows came out at night'.
Alice Little

I had an idea of what it would be like to meet your very own spiritual teacher but I was wrong. I imagined fireworks and a sudden deep connection, but it didn't happen that way. In fact it was quite uneventful, well almost.

The event I attended was over ten days long and when I got there what a shock. The building the retreat was held in was to say the least small! Yet it was packed to the gills with people everywhere. There were queues for everything. You had to queue firstly to take off your shoes and hang up your coat. While you queued on a staircase to do this people were coming up the stairs squashing past to get up while at the same time there seemed to be a queue for the toilets. There was a sense of chaos and dilemma especially from myself who had never been before. There was the usual camaraderie between people who obviously knew each other but for me I felt I knew no one.

I eventually hung up my coat on a rack so groaning with coats that you couldn't find a space in-between. It was also full of people all taking off their shoes and coats together in a very tiny room as well as folk standing having a natter in the midst of it. I had no idea where anything was or what I was supposed to be doing.

Michael Hookham (Rigdzin Shikpo)

This was not my first meeting with Buddhism or meeting a teacher. My first meeting of a teacher was when I went to Oxford to a retreat with students of Rigdzin Shikpo. He was a catalyst to finding my real teacher. My Root Lama

His wife (Shenpen Hookham) was holding the retreat and unknown to me it was a silent retreat. I had a lot of strange experiences on that retreat which now I may consider as being a bit screwy. I kept seeing a horse in my mind running around the room and distracting me especially when I was trying to concentrate. This lasted quite a few days and I'm afraid it made me laugh or smile at strange times. I wonder now if it were my inner child screaming to play rather than sit quietly? Buddhism can certainly make you feel crazy.

Most people at this retreat seemed to know each other and it was a small group, very ordered and peaceful. Held in a lovely woodland setting. The days were structured with meditation at seven in the morning followed by a lovely porridge and stewed fruit breakfast afterwards.

There was a Tai Chi lesson and then teachings. Michael Hookham came on the last day of the retreat and I was quite surprised to see he was English, not having known anything about him and his group before coming. He appeared to be very authentic and relaxed. His story of all the years he spent with Tibetan masters was inspiring to hear.

I decided to try and join a local group from his tradition afterwards and although they were very nice people, they all went down the pub afterwards and it just didn't do it for me.

I had a lot of experiences after the retreat that I wanted some help or advice about because those experiences had created in me such a feeling of panic. But there was no one to talk to about it. If I did try to talk about it no one was interested.

There is a culture in Buddhism that experiences aren't talked about as they are looked on as traps, keeping one hooked on looking for new experiences, which can even be blocks. It's just that when you are new to this stuff you could do with some guidance. I believe Buddhism is the path of self-realisation, the loners path because that's how it has always felt to me. All of us are alone aren't we whatever we do. Each individual having their own little trip inside their head.

I did go to another of Rigdzin Shikpo's talks but there was something missing for me that I couldn't find so I left it there.

Encountering Sufism

'Yesterday I was clever, so I wanted to change the world.
Today I am wise, so I'm changing myself'.
Jalaluddin Rumi

I met Sufism quite by accident. I became very friendly with a girl who had been in a therapy group I belonged to. We would meet regularly and I found her very helpful in that I was able to talk about the problems I was having in my life. She seemed to be a good listener.

I was not aware of narcissism at the time so I did not realise that although she was listening to me she very rarely opened up about herself. Whenever I asked her about herself she would not go very deeply about her past or would change the subject. It is only now that I know that narcissist friends can listen to you for hours, gathering information. They listen to your problems from a power angle of 'you're not ok but they are ok'.

I ignored it when all the things that I was involved in, which she had dismissed and sneered at, became the things that later on she would join, become part of or start to do. Only now do I see that as all narcissists do she was stealing my life.

She appeared so kind and I was so damaged that I thought she was above me and believed that she was much better than I. That was until I became stronger and was changing as I healed.

As I began to heal I noticed how she had started to criticize me. I first had a friendship with her on my own and it seemed fine then when I moved house she came to visit and I was always with my husband and the dynamics changed. She began to move in on my husband very slowly, ingratiating herself with him, knowing that he would not see beyond the mask that I was now seeing for myself. My husband was very naive and kind and she appeared to be so beguiling. It was the little things I noticed at first, the invitations to jealousy that she created, the throwaway comments to belittle me that I knew my husband would not hear. Although I didn't feel that anything untoward would happen on his part, I was aware of her game. She wanted to get between us.

When she started to be unkind to me but kind to him I knew I was in trouble. She was trying to drive a wedge between us and, although our relationship was strong, I trusted my instincts about what was happening. It felt 'off', the dynamics were changing and I saw her for what she was. Life had created a circumstance that helped me to let her go.

When I look back now I see that all the friends I had were narcissists. They used my kind and damaged nature to take from me the little energy I had left to fight. One by one they all fell by the wayside. It was hard to loose so many friends but now I can look back and see them for who they really were and realise I had a lucky escape. They weren't friends at all but I was in such a blinkered and needy place that I did not know they were just using me.

I liked a lot of the teachings of Sufism but found them just a bit too poetic and romantic. The emphasis was very much on love, being in love with the divine, crazy in love, a fool for love. It just wasn't for me. I joined a group and found the people to be very sincere but they went to sleep and that was part of their way which I didn't understand, the way of dreaming and analysing the dreams. I wanted to be awake.

When I made that choice that was the moment I met my teacher.

The cry of a thousand wounds

I came with my damaged wounded self
looking for a fix,
for someone to make me right
and whole again.
I just didn't know
that I had to do that
all by myself.
Sometimes that burden is too great
for a survivor of
Childhood Narcissistic Abuse
already running on empty.

Alice Little

Back to the City retreat….

Buddhism= 'A compass for the bewildered'.
Sogyal Rinpoche.

After I had taken off my shoes and coat I found my way into the shrine room. It was a large, high ceiling room at basement level. What hit me most was the colour. There was yellow, blue, red and gold everywhere and pictures of all sorts of teachers. Having been brought up in a Christian faith where worshipping false gods was out, the brainwashing of my childhood was kicking in as I sought to be alarmed by all the visual imagery.

The teachings I heard that first day from his older students were what I had been searching for for ever. Here was a whole way of understanding what life was about and I felt that I had finally come home. There were a few people that I met at that first retreat, kind, gentle folk and, like me they left one by one many years later. Unable to withstand unkindness that they met within the Sangha.

By lunch time I had a monster headache and approached a member of the care team to ask where could I buy headache tablets who kindly told me 'Why don't you just go through it!'. That was my first meeting with how people use the teachings literally and as an excuse to be unkind. It was a small thing within much of the same thing that happened to me throughout my time with this group.

You see you are supposed to look at all the bad stuff as your Karma or a teaching to help you but then that allows room for unkind folk to beat you up with I and all under the guise of the teachings. If you're not dealing with your stuff or seeing that it is not the other person at fault, but you, you can feel really bad about that.

As someone who was narcissisticly abused by their family you then take on the scapegoat of a group. I got to feel really bad about myself a lot of the time. I just didn't really find that out until I had been in the group for over about 20 years and after a three year retreat. Going no contact with my family and loosing everything woke me up to ALL narcissistic abuse and I had been blind to that happening within my spiritual group because I wrongly assumed we were all on the path of non-harming together.

I'm not saying I was perfect but I now see that I was a bit too kind and a bit too empathetic to survive within a group of strong individuals.

I did a lot of voluntary work which I loved and it gave me a sense of belonging. I wrongly said this to someone else and they set about removing me from the job and taking it for themselves. This happened several times and I found it to be an insidious and unhealthy disease within the organisation.

Eventually I would be relegated to the most menial and loathsome tasks, while trying to be a Buddhist about it through gritted teeth.

Rinpoche did not attend this retreat til later because he had a death in his family and was attending a funeral. Instead his older students were teaching. I don't know what it was about hearing the teachings but I just got a great feeling of love as if my heart had been closed and was now opened.

When Rinpoche did finally arrive I saw him enter the hall and it was as if he were just any other person and it was a bit disappointing. But I had said to myself before he arrived that the teachings were so wonderful that I didn't care who the teacher was I was going to follow him as he must be my teacher. I had no conception at the time about what following a teacher meant, only now do I know. It seems that the flashback I had to my rebirth may be going to happen again in my next life, I hope not, but it all seems to be lining up that way today.

Rinpoche is a great teacher, he knows how to speak to a Western audience and he was also very funny. What he did do, that helped me enormously and still does to this day, was to introduce me to the nature of my mind. This wasn't a one off event but something that happened to both new and old students. It's impossible to describe and it wasn't until I actually left this particular group that I understood what it was I was being introduced to, which is indescribable, without creating room for someone to make concepts about it.

This is just a personal description of what it is to me but even this doesn't fully describe it and I'm sure it's only a glimpse of what it really is to someone much more sorted out than myself.

The nature of mind

If I were to describe it in words I would say that when I'm in it I have space in my mind. It is as if I can look at things without creating a story about what it is I'm looking at yet at the same time I am fully aware of everything. Though even that is momentary as words drift by and take it away. Yet I am not spaced out but absolutely present and aware and alive, I can still see everything clearly and fully.

Beyond this explanation I could only refer you to Chapter 41 of the Tibetan book of Living and Dying, called The Nature of Mind.

On the cushion teaching

'How could you teach me when you weren't even there?
Then I realised the teaching was coming from within
my own wisdom mind'.
Alice Little

My first real life teaching came on my cushion and it was a big surprise. When you are on retreat everything becomes magnified as if real life were in front of you but bigger, bolder and in your face. My usual negativity was that I was always squashed in and at the back and everyone else had more space, especially the girl in front of me. I had no room to move and was rubbing knees and shoulders with people on either side of me. Meanwhile the girl in front had so much room and so much of her stuff around her it looked like she was camping out. She owned that space, unlike me.

I would go in each day and see in front of me her empty space. She was always late and that big space she was taking up got more and more irritating with each day. I wonder if she ever felt my eyes boring into her head. But as the days went by and I started to hear the teachings something shifted inside me. I surrendered. I gave up being annoyed that I had to be squashed in, or move along to let someone else in thereby less space for me. I just gave that up and dropped my whole little shitty trip and breathed.

What happened next was that she disappeared, her place left completely empty with none of her stuff there to hold the space. I watched and looked around waiting for her to return but she didn't and so I realised with a wonderment that that space was mine. No one else was taking it and she wasn't coming back. So I slid right into that space and began to relax and enjoy the retreat. I really, really then appreciated that space.

The next thing that happened was that a rather scruffy bearded man with no socks on was barging in to sit down. He had a huge briefcase and was bashing everyone about including a lady in

211

front of me who was really annoyed by this. I wasn't bothered by him as I was now in chill-out mode so I offered him one of my cushions to sit on but he refused and instead kept bashing against the lady in front, who I now saw reacting in a similar way to how I had been previously. I spoke to her afterwards about the incident and she said to me ' But he had such corny feet!'. I laughed. That's what Buddhism does, makes you laugh at the ridiculousness of yourself and your behaviours.

I was to learn many, many lessons throughout the years but none so direct a teaching as at that time.

Meeting the teachings

*'I didn't know I was looking for myself
but even that I had to give up'.*
Alice Little

To say that I had been looking for these teachings all my life would be an understatement. When I heard them it was as if a big light went on in my head and I was being fed this amazing nectar of dharma that just instantly transformed my mind and being. In simple terms it just made sense of my life when my life wasn't making sense. I knew I had met them before.

Everything that I had been experiencing in my life up to now had a reference. The Dharma (truth) as they call it.

It's not for everyone but most people would be able to relate to many of the Buddhist teachings and certainly the statue of a Buddha does not seem to offend, in fact there are even statues in bars now!

I was a really good student because I knew how to beat myself up and give myself a hard time. The mistake I made was to allow the teachings to make me dull. I gave up my life more and more because that is my habit, that's how I punish myself. I know how to do that. I just needed a stick to help me and Dharma was the stick. It could have been something else, after all I had found many things in the past to stop me, usually partners.

The Buddhist teachings really resonated with me and so I followed and studied with this group for some 20 years. I went on many retreats but the longest was a three year retreat which was the hardest thing I have ever done in my life. It brought my awareness to my depression which I had denied and it also brought my awareness of how bad my childhood had been.

The three year retreat was a really punishing schedule that I had lined up for myself to suffer with. But I don't regret it, it was a once in a lifetime experience and it changed my life. I learned more about myself and my life when I left the retreat because once again my life as I knew it came crashing down around me.

Within a few years, once again, as had happened before in the past, I was to loose everything and would wander into another wilderness of my life and start again.

The covert spiritual narcissistic

He plays the long game
His prey, anyone
who shows a weakness
a neediness
He does not see you,
he only sees his supply.
He is such a junky
for his fix.
He cares
not how or who
he feeds off.
His cover has been achieved
through subterfuge.
While you the victim
have no cover,
only being yourself.
He will break you,
take you, discard you,
and try to destroy you.
The devil dressed in the
clothes of a spiritual seeker.
Forgive yourself if you
have been fooled by this
most evil of brothers

Alice Little

Groomed by the Narcissist

'Once I heard the Pied Pipers flute I followed blindly, I had heard it before'.
Alice Little

Not long before I went on the three year retreat something happened to me that caused me a great deal of shame and disgust. I was groomed by a predatory narcissist. If you have ever been groomed by a narcissist you will understand what I am about to tell you. If you don't understand then I would highly recommend getting to know about this most dangerous personality disorder in case you get caught. I talk about this disorder more in Part 1.

The man who groomed me was known to me, in fact, I had known him for over 10 years before he struck. I had thought of him as a friend and even trusted him. I never saw him as a threat, ever. He was a dharma brother and I wrongly gave too much credence to someone who I thought was walking the path. He appeared to be the kind of man that a woman felt safe to be around. He didn't appear to have any agenda, in fact, he seemed like a really good enthusiastic Buddhist practitioner. Why did that change? What was it that perhaps I was showing that made him think that, after all this time, I was fair game?

He had said at some point that he would like to get an empowerment for a practice we were doing. You get an empowerment in order to gain merit for doing the practice and also you have to have the practice explained. Without this it has no power, hence the word empowerment. So when I found out that there was an empowerment happening in another centre I told him about it. He said he would meet me at the bus stop and I would show him where the centre was.

There were several other people going from our centre as well who I saw there.

When I met him at the bus stop he touched my neck and said that I had cream on it which I hadn't rubbed in. I didn't question that it was a bit intimate and I didn't stop him because it was so quick that I discounted it. We walked to the centre and he sat next to me. I couldn't explain why but I felt he had a hold over me and I felt overpowered by whatever was happening. He disappeared at lunch time and was late getting back and I wondered where he had been. I can guess now that he had been to see a woman or even a prostitute.

When the event had finished we got on the bus and I couldn't work out why he was talking to me as if I were his girlfriend. It was weird and I couldn't even describe now the words he was using. I was not interested in this man but something was happening and it felt out of my control. But I had known him for so long that I was doubting myself because this didn't seem like the man I knew and trusted. This was a stranger that I didn't know.

In a way I had never been alone with him, or I had always been in the centre with him with others around. Maybe something had happened to him in his life to make him change. Or perhaps he had always been like this and I had never noticed.

Alters

Looking at my background of abuse I can see now that he was possibly accessing one of my (alters). I describe this in Part 2. Just to repeat that when you have been sexually abused as a child you often split off from the abuse so that you don't feel the pain, then that pain is held in a part of you that you may or may not be able to access later on. In ritual abuse alters are specifically created to use at a later stage, sometimes unknown to the person. I don't know how he was doing this, perhaps it was something he was doing that was familiar to that part of me that was hidden but it didn't make sense to me at the time.

I sort of blank out here because I don't know how he managed to get me meeting him, I just don't remember. I do know that he was waiting at the bus top I was at when on my way to the centre and now I realise that he was waiting for me, knowing which train I would arrive on. He suggested walking and instead of the usual route which was on a busy road he said he knew a short cut. So I

217

went with him. It wasn't a short cut at all but a deserted footpath along a river. He made me sit down and then proceeded to feel my breasts asking me to show them to him.

Afterwards I was so disgusted at myself and I wasn't interested in him nor attracted to him yet I felt I was powerless to say no to this man. He was accessing a really crazy inside part of me that was leading me into danger. Now that I recount it I see that when I was groomed as a child it was so similar.

Then one day I finally woke up. The reason I woke up was that he was now escalating what he wanted, into full sex by asking me to stay in a hotel with him and making a date to do so.

I didn't want to go to the hotel with him, in fact I was terrified so I decided to tell my husband because by now I was in such a state. I had no idea how my husband would react. Although I was not interested in this man nonetheless I had to take some responsibility for allowing it to go so far.

I did tell my husband and he supported me with it, even coming to the centre with me one day in case this guy started something because I hadn't gone to the hotel to meet him. I changed my phone number and the only time I spoke to him after that was when he came up to me and said 'what happened to you?' and I told him I wasn't interested. His reply was 'well when you're finished with me you're finished, there is no going back'. Like we were having a relationship?

It took me a very long time to get over this abusive episode because that is what happened, I was abused by a narcissist. No it wasn't a normal sexual attraction, nor a normal affair, it was a grooming by an adult paedophile and I had been the target. I hate to imagine what would have happened if I had gone to that hotel, it just doesn't bear thinking about.

He dirtied my visits to the centre and I never felt comfortable there ever again if he was there.

After this incident was over I started to watch him and also looked back at how he had got to me, because I realised that I wasn't the only one he was grooming. He would often do strange things like be secretly intimate with other women and there were several of them, yet no one would have guessed. If I had told anyone, no one would have believed me.

If you had seen his moves you wouldn't know what he was up to, you would just ignore it as being friendly, but it wasn't. I did tell one woman about what was happening and I know that she didn't really understand what I was telling her because as I was crying and telling her she said 'your just a bit needy'. I found the use of the word a bit strange even if it were true and many years later I noticed that she also was in his sights. I reminded her what I had said to her to warn her, I don't know if she listened.

However she did tell me of two other women who had complained that he had kissed them out of the blue. One of them I remember as a lady who he had hung around with a lot and at the time I didn't question it, I thought they were just friends. Just as no one would have questioned his friendship with me. He would have relied on others ignoring this. Both of those ladies left the centre and never came back. I too left the centre but it wasn't because of him. What an absolute toad he is. The problem is that he was very well thought of as a good student, very helpful and also gave money to the centre regularly.

I wonder now what else goes on there that I never saw.

I lost trust in the people around me and I questioned their motives. I was waking up even then but not fully. After that day I never let another man come near me in that place and there may have been many who were above board but I didn't care because I didn't want to be lured by yet another narcissist. I was starting to learn their devious ways, yet I still had a long way to go.

This happening was nothing to do with Buddhism but rather of my own ignorance and abuse from childhood but mainly because this man was a predatory man who had been and most probably is still ignored or abetted.

Being a Buddhist is not about letting people walk all over you and I had to leave this group to fully understand what that meant because I misunderstood that and I realise that it allowed space for abuse or being taken advantage of because of an empathetic nature.

My easy going, kind and open nature was an invitation throughout my life to be abused and used by both men and women. Eventually you wake up and then you shut off and become closed. You have to go through that process so you can heal and learn to create healthy boundaries when needed without shutting off anything good that may come your way.

Finding loneliness

In a desolate place
with all distractions
removed,
I found the meaning of
utter,
complete,
loneliness
and from that loneliness,
concentration arose.
Looking for something.
I had instead,
found nothing,
seeing nothing,
I saw indeed.

Alice Little

The three year retreat

'You don't let go of life, you let go of attachment, yearning and grasping.'
Sogyal Rinpoche

There are defining moments in one's life, milestones along the way when you can say 'Ah yes that was an adventure!'. For me a defining time was when I entered a three year mountain retreat.

When one mentions the word retreat to a person who has never been on one, an image is conjured up of spas and saunas and relaxation. A spiritual retreat is not like that, it's quite the opposite. You go on retreat to give up your ego, not to get something and, therefore, when the things that held the ego together are stripped apart, it hurts. It is a small death. You wonder why anyone would want to go on retreat, but, I guess you never think it is going to be as bad as it is. I had been on two week retreats and they were manageable though tough, yet I felt good afterwards.

On retreat everything is magnified. All the things you avoid in life come up to be looked at and purified and in a long retreat like this you can barely imagine how hard it was. This is the fast track and you have to pay for it.

I had known about the retreat for years, as I heard people planning how they would manage attending it, but I never really thought it would be for me, only people better than me. So I brushed it to one side until a second invitation came for me to join it when it was almost about to start.

There was a terrible urge in me to go to this retreat now that years had passed, possibly because I was ready. But it wasn't that easy to go for many reasons. The first one was that the team running it wanted to make sure that you really wanted to go and so I presumed that I wouldn't be going. I was surprised then to get an invitation to join it and then I was left to sort out the practical side of things which was much worse. In doing this I had no support whatsoever to organise this and I didn't know who to ask.

Certainly no one asked me how I was doing with anything practical. I had to do everything alone as usual.

How does one take three years out of one's life and have a life to come back to? Or do you just go and worry about that after you leave the retreat?

My main attachment and responsibility in my life was my husband. I also had a business. The business I had to give up and would then have to survive as well as possible on my savings, which would run out very quickly.

My husband has always been very supportive of my growth but I thought this might be a step too far. After I told him it was a possibility I could go on this retreat he didn't try to stop me nor discourage me instead I think he kept any fears of his own to himself so that I could go.

It seemed that I was now considering such a selfish-self indulgent thing. When something calls you, you just have to go and this was calling me. In a way I didn't really think it out, had not visualised day to day what it would be like and didn't know either. I also didn't think about what it would be like for my husband without me practically, though I knew we would miss each other. I didn't realise or think about exactly how much this would affect both of us.

Because I had joined the retreat late, along with a few other people, I found out that there was no room for me on-site. I would have to find a place to stay off-site and it was only a month away! The mountains were inhospitable, sparsely populated and very damp though beautiful. There were very few houses nearby.

I had to share a house with several other people and that was in itself awful. Three other people who were all on retreat, all working out their own things was a recipe for disaster. Living off-site was a disaster and everything in-between was a disaster too, including myself.

The first week was just an adjustment to living in retreat and how that would be. There was a schedule which started with practice then teachings and in between there was lunch, tea breaks and dinner. It was relaxed at the beginning but that soon ended.

The teachings themselves were utterly amazing and I am so glad that I was able to be there at that time to hear them. It's just that the rest of it I found difficult.

The worst part was missing my husband. I missed him more almost more than he missed me. He was still living in our house with everything familiar around him, though without me. I experienced really deep grief at not being around him every day because we had been so close for so long. That was something I think I never really adjusted to but I wasn't the only one by a long shot.

There were people from all over the world attending the retreat, of all ages. Some had left partners, some families and jobs and others had left their children to be here. You would think that with all these people together that it would be exciting and party-like but I have never felt so alone than I did among those 500 people who were on retreat beside me. It was the loneliest time in my life.

It was during the retreat that I finally admitted and realised that I had serious depression because I went into a serious dive into depression and mental unhealth while I was there. I was in retreat with 500 people who all had problems of their own, some worse than mine.

As I recall that time and the events I realise that I was in great danger from my own mind and I was lucky that I had the strength not to commit suicide or go crazy. I was in retreat to become healthy in my mind, to discover what my mind was and how to train it. I didn't realise how bad my mind was. I was lonely and wanted to go home and they told me I would feel that way. Some people even did go home, there was nothing to stop you, you weren't locked in. I had given up so much to be there and leaving, although tempting, wasn't an option.

When I went into retreat I didn't know how low I was or that I could get even lower. As the time went on and I saw how awful and unkind people were being I retreated more and more into myself.

I couldn't stand living with the people in the house so I had to make a decision to live on my own, though more expensive. I also had to buy a car as everyone who had a car was already giving lifts to others and I found myself stranded one day unable to get to the retreat, I just sat and cried. So I took the decision to buy a car, another great expense. The main problem with that was that all of a sudden I was everyone's favourite person as they all wanted lifts, only they didn't want to help with the petrol and that really got to me.

If you had a button to push on retreat you could guarantee it would get pushed and mine did again and again. I was to get lonelier and lonelier. I found that I adhered to the silence which we were supposed to keep to create a retreat atmosphere yet most didn't. It exaggerated my loneliness as I saw people at lunch and tea chatting away to each other as if they were on holiday. Being quiet wasn't a problem for me but being on my own in a large group of people was.

You get used to being on retreat and that's when the rug is pulled from under you and you feel shaken up by anything that changes. The idea is to mirror life. We do not see that there is a constant change over and over, each day, each minute it is changing and we are experiencing loss, but we don't see it. On retreat you see it glaringly and its painful.

Being high up in the mountains meant that the weather changed a lot, it could be very hot and sunny or heavy rain and thunderstorms. In the winter it was an amazing snow scene but very cold. Driving away from the centre was hazardous especially in the dark and rain and especially in a thunderstorm because you were, in fact, driving through a cloud that high up.

My biggest hang up was that I felt no one liked me and everyone avoided me. In fact one unkind soul told me that when he saw me arriving on that first day he didn't like the look of me but could now see I was a really nice person. He did this because he had had a teaching on confession and had taken it literally. Projecting his own inferiority on me, he gave a compliment and then took it back. It wasn't true that no one liked me because a few people did. I think it's just that I'm told I look very self-contained and not wanting of anything. How wrong can people be.

There were indeed some very unkind people on retreat and as my own personal stuff was revealed for me, they also had to deal with their monster and a few really did become monsters. Myself included.

We were told at the very beginning what it could be like for us on a long retreat and that certainly was coming true. Without the distractions of everyday life you start to latch on to anything to distract you, mostly other people's irritating habits. I learned a lot about myself and I definitely came away with something that I feel has never left me.

I met many great teachers on this retreat, too many to list but among them were: The Dalai Lama, Mingyur Rinpoche, Tsoknyi Rinpoche, Garchen Rinpoche, Dzigar Kontrul Rinpoche and others. The teachings we got from these amazing Tibetans was the best part of the retreat. It was the one time I could sit for hours listening. In the end though you have to apply the teachings to yourself. Just listening passively is not enough and applying the teachings to yourself is hard, very hard.

On the very last day of the retreat there was a party but I left before it had finished. It was dark and I had no car by then and there was no one else leaving to give me a lift. So I just stood and looked up at the sky. Because of the lack of light pollution the sky was covered in amazing bright and clear stars, thousands of them and it was the most beautiful sight I have seen of a sky before or after that time. It was such a beautiful ending to the retreat and it stays with me always. Unable to get home and telling myself off for leaving the party early, I just surrendered to the moment and sat down and gave up. As is often the case when we surrender we get what we want. I was lucky that another couple in a car were leaving too and I left the retreat with just a glance back and a farewell. Happy to leave and go home, yet sad to leave what I had come to know as my spiritual home. What a journey it had been.

Reality checks

If I were you
and you were me
I would have made
great effort
to encourage me
to remain.
Instead I found that
you didn't care
for your dharma sister
when she needed you.
When I had cared
for so many of you.
This was not Buddhist practice,
this was just neglect.

Alice Little

Leaving my Buddhist Group

Once the Buddha and Ananda visited a monastery where a monk was suffering from a contagious disease. The poor man lay in a mess with no one to look after him. The Buddha himself washed the sick monk and placed him in a new bed. Afterwards, he admonished the other monks. "Monks you have neither mother nor father to look after you. If you do not look after each other who will look after you? Whoever serves the sick and suffering serves me".

As with anything else in this mortal life I found out that my perception of Buddhists was totally mis-informed including the way I thought of myself as a Buddhist. I had looked on Buddhists as being peaceful, loving, kind, non-violent folk and they were but also many were quite the opposite because they were human. So I began to realise that the role of Buddhism was to '**Practice** non-violence and peace'. While the people within it were **training** to be such a person. For everyone it's a hard journey and we are all trying to constantly train and watch our minds to remove the harm within us. It is difficult to be a good human being, a truly good human being.

It's a shock to find out that your fairy tale concept of Buddhism has been removed and harsh reality has taken its place.

After the three year retreat had ended and I went back to normal life, so to speak, my world began to fall apart. Nothing can prepare you for what it is like to leave a long term retreat. That in itself was the biggest come down of all and I wasn't ready for it or had any idea what it would mean.

Some time soon after the end of the retreat I made contact with my parents again. My heart had been softened with all the teachings and I was hoping to make everything right again. I found that they soon began their usual unkind tirade on me and this time I walked away. I had no choice but to go No Contact with them.

I wrongly thought that I would be able to turn to the Sangha for help but there was no help there. I tried to explain what I was going through but I knew that no one really understood. My words were falling on deaf ears and I was becoming more and more needy by their lack of support.

One particular person, who was supposed to be part of the care system they had in place, as well as ignoring my pleas for support, almost seemed to be needling me and making it worse.

Many, many things happened at that time which showed me that they just didn't care, that you are on your own. One of them was that they actually took me off the main data base used for the whole of the sangha, as if I didn't exist any more. When all I had asked them to do was take me off the data base of a small local centre I was visiting at the time because I was no longer able to attend there. That in itself felt like a slap in the face. It took me a long time to realise that they were not going to help me in my suffering and so I just stopped going.

Unfortunately there are narcissists within Buddhism and I met them of course. Why would it be any different than it was in the outside world? The only thing I can say on leaving was that it wasn't a cult because no one tried to persuade me to stay. I did get a call from one of Rinpoche's older students who instead of asking me how I was, pretended they were calling to ask me about advice on the town I was living in and that, in itself, I found deeply unsympathetic.

I had also moved a long way from any centre I could visit easily and together with the cost of travelling to a centre I now realised that I had to make a decision to leave. Everything that was happening was leading towards this decision, I was feeling pushed out and so I left and became a lone yogi.

I knew that this was just a group thing, a human thing because I remembered on the three year retreat that Rinpoche was alarmed that about 150 people had left. He asked all the older students to contact these people and ask them why they had left and what could they do to address any problems. So I know that being left just to leave as I did was not his teaching, but rather a human failing and a bad one.

I knew the story of Milarepa who was a great yogi and saint from the 10th century. His teacher made him build a tower and re-build it again five times so that he could work with his ego. I loved his story of transformation but I felt I couldn't live up to be the person Milarepa was. I felt I had already had my ego very much subdued by my narcissist parents and that I needed to be built up rather than taken apart. My Milarepa teaching, I felt, had happened at my parent's feet and I couldn't imagine how much more of my ego was left to destroy. I know it's a very subtle and tricky thing, ego, and so I ended up feeling that I had no sense of myself good or bad in the end.

When I finally left the group I was an empty shell, beaten by life and an abusive family and now it felt also by my spiritual brothers and sisters. I had lost everything once again.

The Lone Yogi

'We are all Buddha's but our Buddha nature has been temporarily obscured. Once the obscurations has been removed, we are Buddha's indeed'
Dharma.

In reality we are never alone and independent because we rely on so many other factors to live. The people who make our food, supply our energy and of course our reliance on this earth and the very air we breath.

Just examining a cup of coffee and seeing how it was brought to you involves a huge team of people as well as your Barista! It is a great exercise to take each item you eat or wear and ask yourself, who was involved in the making of this? You can see an interconnection with many, many others who have touched your life each day, unseen. So our life is a series of interdependent actions with another, though we may never see them, we rely on them none the less.

It has taken me all my life to accept myself for who I am and that is, I am a loner, an interdependent loner!

Spending all my childhood in isolation from others was certainly a start to that. My abusive childhood was a training course in how to keep away from others while remaining within the abusive family as a so called safe place, according to them. This isolating from others is what an abusive family will often do. Then finding narcissistic partners to further validate this by keeping me tied to them and isolated from having friends.

I know now that it is too late in life to become the life and soul of the party, nor would I want to. I have however become a good friend to myself and being alone I know now is not the same as being lonely. I have experienced the worst loneliness ever while on my three year retreat and I was among 500 people.

I have learned through Buddhism that fighting suffering makes it worse and having an aversion to it attracts it. Over time and having no choice because of life events I have made peace with

231

my aloneness. I am, in fact, becoming grateful for the bliss of peace in being alone. In doing so I no longer feel lonely, in fact, I revel in being alone.

When I left my abusive family I had to also leave everything and everyone I knew in order to break that cycle of abuse. It left me in an incredibly lonely place, which I had to make peace with, in order to survive. I have to have hope that this may not always be so, but for now it is my path.

Society is not geared towards the acceptance of loners. People who commit crimes are often described as loners as if it were unacceptable. While loners feel less than because they choose not to be part of the crowd. It's ok to be **alone** but I found that **loneliness** was different and usually part of depression and now that depression has lifted from me I find that loneliness has also lifted.

We never know where life will take us and I am always open to change but I think after all this time I would miss being a lone yogi.

When the 3 year retreat had ended my teacher said that in this age of the Kaliyuga, "the dregs of time", when emotions and all of life becomes grosser, you, the lineage holders of this Dzogchen tradition are as good as it gets. While he, as our teacher, is also a sign of these degenerate times. I would agree with that. Certainly the bit about myself as a lineage holder.

He also said:"I have given you everything, more I can not give, now it's up to you".

You see we all want to be spoon fed everything, including enlightenment. We want maximum effect with little effort and that's me. It seems so much easier to spend hours on the internet or reading novels or aimlessly thinking than making an effort to train my mind. While, all the time, death closes in.

I know how to train my mind, I know its tricks and how it works, yet still I follow it's bad advice daily and ignore the duller mind instead of listening to the wisdom mind that repeatedly says to me WAKE UP!!! Teaching is certainly not my skill and I really have a bad memory and a poor use of vocabulary so all I can tell you is how to meditate. You have to start with meditation to still your busy mind and you also have to end everything with meditation. It is a skill you can practice but it's not easy, however, the rewards are enormous.

I certainly would not teach the dharma to anyone because I don't feel I have the capacity. I don't have any visions of myself as anything special so I can at least thank my abusive parents for giving me too much humility! All I can do is tell you about my life because my life is a teaching for myself. Who knows, it may resonate with someone.

I can tell you how to meditate though because I'm sure I won't make too many mistakes with that. However an introduction to the nature of your mind by a teacher who has realised theirs is the only way you can deepen your meditation and go beyond. So that meditation is your life and not just something you do on a cushion. You will have to find a teacher and tradition that suits you should you choose a spiritual path.

Like any skill you have to learn, meditation is something that you become familiar with over time. Learning the pitfalls of meditation is something I was taught while on my three year retreat and if you get used to meditation you may consider looking for a teacher. However, I would advise discretion in who you choose, checking them out as much as you can while also not being put off by stories you may hear about them. Sometimes crazy teachers are hard to understand but the effort could be well worth it.

You can't always tell who a yogi is by how they look. Sometimes they look crazy. They could also just look like an ordinary person who you don't even notice. They may even have very bad faults! That's mainly because many yogis are hidden, or hide their realisations. So if you are looking for a teacher it's your job to check them out. Just make sure you don't pass one over by making a concept of what a yogi looks like. Or worse still go for the personality, cult teachers and be led astray. That can damage you for years.

233

How to meditate

'Meditation is the state of non-distraction'.
Dharma

Meditation is seen as a way to be peaceful and yes, a benefit of it is a peaceful mind but it is more than that. Meditation is actually getting to know yourself in a most profound way. This means that you will get to know yourself on many levels and not all of them are peaceful, some are challenging.

In this type of meditation from the Tibetan Buddhist tradition, you keep your eyes open. If you find this too difficult at first begin the meditation with your eyes closed for a few seconds before you open them.

Environment

To inspire yourself to meditate you need to create the right environment to make it more conducive for meditation to arise.

Body on your cushion
Mind in your body

The outer environment is created to inspire your senses and you can do this by creating a shrine or just simply a place you always go to meditate. Then as soon as you sit in this special place your mind and body become accustomed to knowing that meditation happens here, it is a reminder. The place you meditate in as far as possible should be quiet and peaceful if you are a beginner.

The inner environment is resting your mind.

There is no pre-requisite to belonging to a religion in order to meditate. Meditation belongs to everyone.

Posture

To inspire your mind to meditate create the right posture before you meditate. You can meditate on a cushion, on the floor, or on a seat if this is more comfortable for you. Lying down is not advised as it is too easy to sleep but if that is the only way you can be because of illness then, if you do fall asleep, as soon as you awake just remember to meditate.

Your spine should be straight like a pile of gold coins one on top of the other. You can sit in a half lotus position with legs crossed or a full lotus if you are able to hold that pose. Your chin should be just slightly tucked in.

Open your mouth only to the point that it is similar to holding a grain of rice between your lips. Your eyes should be placed so that you are looking slightly down your nose without fixating, keeping the eyes relaxed and soft. Place your hands palm down upon your knees gently and slowly resting them there.

There should be some space between your arm and your armpit so that your arms are not gripping tightly against your body. This posture is like an eagle about to fly. The breathing is natural and not forced, there is just an awareness of your breathing in and out.

Creating the right environment and the posture will seem a bit forced at first. I have a tendency to fidget so it was never easy. When I did stay still I found that I was too rigid and hard on myself and I could sit for ages though not be actually meditating.

So we have now created the right environment and posture and we are sitting on our cushion or chair. Everything seems peaceful but then you notice that your thoughts have proliferated and become even worse and you can even feel like giving up. Don't! Because this means you are getting somewhere as you now have noticed how much you think. Before you were always busy and didn't notice your thoughts and now you see them because the body is still.

You can not stop the mind from thinking but you can stop the mind from following each thought and creating stories. As soon as you have a thought instead of trying to stop thinking, look at the thought and see it but don't follow it up, don't start thinking about the thought. It is just a thought. If it helps you can label it, as just a 'thought'. Your thoughts should be like watching trains go through a station.

If you do find it difficult to meditate by just sitting you can use an object as a support for your meditation practice. The object can be as simple as a pebble or a candle. When you lose concentration you bring your attention back the object. You can also use your breath as a support and whenever you become distracted you place your mind on the breath, very lightly, watching the breath go in and out. Not trying to breathe but rather watching the natural flow of the breath.

Your mind will race at first but eventually with practice your mind will become more pliable and still. It will take time and patience to master this practice but once you do you will be able to meditate anywhere even in a busy place with lots of noise and distraction. But first you need to find a quiet space so that meditation can arise naturally away from the business of your life.

Meditation has helped me enormously though I found it hard at first, having been made to sit so still as a child it felt like a punishment. I can now usually meditate more easily whenever I choose to and still my mind. Some days I have to make more effort if my mind is racing and untamed.

You can also do walking meditation where you walk slowly one foot in front of the other with your eyes slightly down and become aware of each step on the earth while remembering to breath and being aware of the thinking mind. I believe that meditation is the greatest gift you can give yourself.

Where I am now

'Looking for the end of your journey is like looking for the end of space'.
Alice Little

My mind is clearer than it has ever been in the whole of my life. My mental health has improved a lot and I am calmer and happier, which seems a paradox because my life is beyond simple. I feel as if I am on a retreat but this time the retreat is life, there is no separation. I have no social life, no car, no income as yet (thanks for buying this book!) and no friends apart from my husband. I have no contact with anyone from my past and yet I am strangely content. However I am open to change

I will forever be grateful to Sogyal Rinpoche and all the other great teachers I met from that Tibetan Buddhist lineage for introducing me to the real nature of my mind. Without that knowledge I could not make sense of the suffering in this world, my own or others. Without it I would have committed suicide a long time ago and it was a thought I lived with most days. That part of me deep inside stopped me every time from using that most violent of escape plans. 'The Wisdom of No Escape' as Pema Chodren poses it. My wisdom mind all the time helping me, leading me, warning me and finally, loving me. Sometimes the chatter of life can make it such a dim voice.

Buddhism taught me so much about myself and so much about life. It gave me an understanding of how life works and has helped me to come to terms with the suffering of my life. Looking at the whole of life as a big training ground I realise that as a child I knew this and that helped me. Whenever I feel I don't understand my life or I need some guidance I always look to the Buddhist teachings and it helps me to put it all in context.

I have been through many, many years of abuse with those close to me and because of this have learned to be a good friend to myself so being alone is not a problem. As the years go by I trust I will find what course my life will take. For now I write

237

most days and listen to teachings on my iPod as well as reading. I can't see myself returning to the Buddhist group I was with.

When I met Buddhism I gave up my life. I stopped reading anything but Dharma and I stopped enjoying life. I knew how to use the Dharma in that way, to be harsh on myself. I just didn't know I was doing it. But spiritual life must be part of what you do every day, it can't be separate. Just at first you do have to separate it by going on retreat. You can still enjoy life. So I'm re-learning how to live again but sometimes I feel that its very late in life to start.

I don't regret anything I've done in my life because it has taught me so much and I didn't know any other way to be than the way I was. All I want to do now is to bring some light on my experience of life and how I got through the bad stuff, how it didn't break me.

I want to take back the realisation that I'm strong, that I can make a difference in this world even in my very small way. If I can do it by writing then that is my way. Speaking never was. We never know who we may have touched, or who we may touch in the future. It may not even happen until after we die. So I reach out now and touch you with my words because at the end of the day that's my medium. We will never meet but you will know me through my words. Words that you may never hear me utter if we were to meet.

I'm a very deep person, too deep for the pleasantries that one has to give on first meeting. So here in print I can be myself and I have opened my heart and mind for you to see me, vulnerable and honest in my story, as much as I can tell without identifying myself so that I can remain free of my abusive past and live in peace at last. This is a story that anyone who met me would not know about me. But you dear reader, you know me.

So if you have managed to read this far thank you for staying the course. I hope it has given you an insight into the life of a spiritual being, a lone yogi and a person who does not follow the crowd. I wish you luck on your journey.

My light can not be dimmed

My light can not be dimmed,
many, many others have tried.
I too have tried.
It is like an everlasting light
that burns eternally.
I could not extinguish it because
it is a lamp in the darkness,
a guiding light
to guide myself
and others through
the dark forest of life
and into the
open pastures
of freedom
where narcissists dare not go
for fear of being blinded.
It has no name this light,
it has no owner, no religion,
it can not be bought and sold
nor exchanged.
But you will know it.
I pass on this light
to you.
Keep it burning.

Alice Little

The Four Noble Truths
The first teaching of the Buddha

The truth of suffering
The truth of the cause of suffering
The truth of the cessation of suffering
The truth of the path to the cessation of suffering

Dear Reader

I hope that you found something in this book that helped you along your path to well being. For me that would make it all worth while, that you, the reader, were able to be touched by something, even by my pain and my healing. To realise that you can move on, that life changes and each moment is an opportunity for transformation.

You didn't know me at the beginning of this book but you may know me a little better now. I wonder that a complete stranger could pick up my book and read it and we could meet in this way mind to mind, it's surreal.

If you did enjoy the book please consider leaving a review online. Thank you in advance for helping me to promote my books so that it may help to touch other people's lives.

It's been a privilege sharing my journey with you.

Goodbye until we meet again

Love Alice

Suggested reading

Here are a just few books that I have read along the way. The whole list would be too long to print!

Self development

What do you say after you say hello? By Eric Berne
I'm ok your ok by Thomas A Harris
Seized by Eve Laplant
The Courage to heal by Ellen Bass and Laura Davis
The autobiography of Malcolm X with Alex Haley
The wheel of life by Elizabeth Kubler- Ross.
The nice girl syndrome by Beverly Engel
Betrayal Trauma by Jennifer J Freyd
Writing down the bones by Natalie Goldberg
The Dance by Oriah Mountain Dreamer
Post Traumatic stress by Glen R Shiraldi
The 33 strategies of war by Robert Green
Maps to Ecstasy by Gabriel Roth
The Call by Oriah Mountain Dreamer
Women who run with the wolves by Clarissa Pinkola Estes
Drawing on the right side of the brain by Betty Edwards
Highly intuitive people by Heidi Sawyer
The stormy search for the self by Christina and Stanislav Grof

Buddhism For Beginners

The Tibetan Book of Living and Dying by Sogyal Rinpoche
Openness, clarity and sensitivity by Michael Hookham
The miracle of mindfulness by Thich Nhat Hanh
Transforming the mind by the Dalai Lama
Loving kindness by Sharon Salzberg
Books by Pema Chodren;
When things fall apart
The wisdom of no escape

242

Start where you are

Buddhism for older students

The words of my perfect teacher by Patrul Rinpoche
Dzogchen the self perfected state by Chogyal Namkai Norbu
Contemplating reality by Andy Karr
Cave in the snow by Vicki Mackenzie
Cutting through spiritual materialism by Chogyam Trungpa

Buddhism for questioning Buddhist or Buddhist atheists

Siddhartha by Herman Hess
After the ecstasy the laundry by Jack Kornfield
Books by Stephen Batchelor;
Buddhism without beliefs
Confessions of a Buddhist atheist
Alone with others

Death

Peaceful death, joyful rebirth by Tulku Thondrup
Facing death and finding hope by Christine Longaker
The wheel of life by Elizabeth Kubler Ross

28239762R00144

Printed in Great Britain
by Amazon